Finance unleashed

Unlocking the wealth and financial freedom

Gold Harbor

Copyright© 2024 by GOLD HARBOR

All rights reserved. No part of this publication may be reproduced, distributed, or transmitted in any form or by any means, including photocopying, recording, or other electronic or mechanical methods, without the prior written permission of the publisher, except in the case of brief quotations embodied in critical reviews and certain other noncommercial uses permitted by copyright law.

Title: FINANCE UNLEASHED

Author: Gold Harbor

Publication Year: 2024

For permission requests, contact the publisher at
ikhlafi1014@gmail.com

TABLE OF CONTENTS

INTRODUCTION	**9**
Chapter 1: Understanding the Financial Mindset	**11**
Sub-chapter 1: The Influence of Mindset	11
• Shift in perspective	11
• Case Studies	12
• Action Steps:	13
Sub-chapter 2: Overcome Financial Limiting Beliefs	14
• Identifying beliefs	14
• Debunking Myths	14
• Reprogramming Strategies	15
Subchapter 3: Developing a Wealth Mindset	17
• Understanding Wealth: Redefining Beyond Monetary Aspect	17
• Visualization Techniques	18
• Implementing Wealth Habits	20
Sub-chapter 4: Embracing Risk and Opportunity	22
• Risk Perception	22
• Balancing Risks	23
• Seizing Opportunities	25
Sub-chapter 5: Mastering the Art of Patience	27
• Delayed Gratification	27
• Long-Term Vision: Stories of Success	

Through Patience 28
- Practical Patience Techniques: Cultivating Patience In Financial Endeavors 28

Chapter 2: Strategic Savings and Spending **31**

Sub-Chapter 1: The Saving Mindset 31
- Importance of Savings 31
- Automated Saving 32
- Emergency Funds: Beyond Expenses and Income 33

Sub-chapter 2: Creating a Budget That Works 34
- Holistic Budgeting 34
- Expense Tracking: Tools and Strategy 35

Subchapter 3: Mindful Spending 37
- Conscious Consumption 37
- Value-Based Spending 38
- Cutting superfluous expenses 39

Sub-chapter 4: Power of Compounding 41
- Compounding 41
- Investing strategy 42
- Time as a partner 43

Sub-chapter 5: Advanced Savings and Investing Techniques 44
- Tax-Efficient Strategies 44
- Diversification 45
- Leveraging Financial Instruments 45

Chapter 3: Maximizing Income Streams **47**

Sub-chapter 1: Beyond 9–5 47
- Side Hustles 47
- Freelancing Opportunities 48

- Passive Income Streams — 49
- Sub-chapter 2: Negotiation Mastery — 49
  - Wage Negotiation — 49
  - Contract Negotiation — 50
  - Negotiation Psychology — 51
- Sub-chapter 3: Entrepreneurial Ventures — 52
  - Identifying Opportunities — 52
  - Startup Strategies — 53
  - Risk Management in Entrepreneurship — 54
- Sub-chapter 4: Investing in yourself — 55
  - Continuous Learning — 55
  - Professional Networking — 56
  - Personal Branding — 57
- Sub-Chapter 5: Achieving Financial Independence — 59
  - FIRE Movement — 59
  - Calculating the FI Number — 60

Chapter 4: Mastering Investment Strategies — 61
- Sub-chapter 1: Risk-Adjusted Returns — 61
  - Risk-Return Tradeoff — 61
  - Asset Allocation — 62
  - Understanding Market Cycles — 63
- Sub-Chapter 2: Behavioral Finance — 64
  - Psychology and Investing — 64
  - Overcoming Cognitive Biases — 65
  - Long-Term Investing Mindset — 65
- Sub-Chapter 3: Alternative Investment — 67
  - Real Estate Investing — 67
  - Cryptocurrency and Blockchain — 68
  - Precious metals and commodities — 69

Sub-chapter 4: Income-generating investments — 70
- Dividend Stocks — 70
- Bonds and Fixed-Income Investments — 71
- REITs and MLPs — 72

Sub-Chapter 5: Sustainable and Socially Responsible Investment — 73
- ESG Criteria — 73
- Impact Investing — 74
- Key strategies include — 75

Chapter 5: Understanding Debt and Credit — 77

Subchapter 1: Understanding Debt — 77
- Types of Debt — 77
- Debt Repayment Strategies — 78
- Debt Consolidation and Refinancing: — 79

Subchapter 2: Building and Maintaining Credit — 80
- Credit scores — 80
- Credit Building Strategies — 81
- Credit Monitoring Tools — 82

Sub-Chapter 3: Smart borrowing — 83
- Loan review — 83
- Interest Rate Negotiation — 84
- Leveraging Credit for Investments — 85

Subchapter 4: Debt-Free Strategies — 86
- Debt Snowball vs. Debt Avalanche — 86
- The Psychology of Debt Freedom — 87
- Creating a Debt-Free Plan — 87

Sub-chapter 5: Credit and Identity Theft Prevention — 89

- Credit Freeze and Monitoring — 89
- Identity Theft Resolution — 89
- Legal Protections: Explore the Legal Tools — 90

Chapter 6: Tax Efficiency and Wealth Preservation — **92**

Sub-Chapter 1: Understanding Tax Systems — 92
- Tax Basics — 92
- Tax Deductions and Credits — 93
- Tax-Advantaged Accounts — 93

Sub-Chapter 2: Tax Planning Strategies — 95
- Year-round Tax Planning — 95
- Professional Assistance — 96
- Tax-Efficient Withdrawal Strategies — 96

Subchapter 3: Estate Planning — 98
- Importance of Estate Planning — 98
- Wills and Trusts — 98
- Legacy Planning — 99

Sub-Chapter 4: Wealth Transfer Strategies — 100
- Gifting Strategies — 100
- Charitable Giving — 101
- Succession Planning for Businesses — 101

Sub-chapter 5: Protecting Wealth During Economic Downturns — 102
- Diversification for Stability — 102
- Insurance as a precaution — 103
- Emergency Funds for Economic Resilience — 104

Chapter 7: Behavioral Finance Mastery — **106**

Subchapter 1: Emotional Intelligence in Finance — 106

- Emotional Resilience — 106
  - Managing Fear and Greed — 107
  - Mindfulness techniques — 108

Sub-chapter 2: Setting and Achieving Financial Goals — 109
- SMART objectives — 109
- Goal Visualization — 110
- Goal tracking and modifications: — 111

Subchapter 3: Behavioral Biases and Investment Pitfalls — 112
- Common Biases — 112
- Avoiding Investment Pitfalls — 113
- Learning from Mistakes: — 113

Subchapter 4: Decision-Making Frameworks — 114
- Cost-Benefit Analysis — 114
- Pros and drawbacks Methodology — 114
- Seeking professional assistance — 115

Sub-chapter 5: Wealth Mindset Maintenance — 115
- Regular Financial Check-ins: — 115
- Adapting to Change — 116
- Appreciating achievements — 117

Chapter 8: Legacy-Building and Impactful Wealth — 118

Sub-Chapter 1: Personal Legacy — 118
- Legacy Beyond Wealth — 118
- Impact on Community — 118
- Balancing Family and Legacy Objectives — 119

Sub-chapter 2: Philanthropic and Social

Impact	120
• Strategic Philanthropy	120
• Creating Social Change	120
• Measuring charitable Impact	121
Sub-Chapter 3: Sustainable and Ethical Investment	122
• Aligning Investments with Values	122
• Supporting Sustainable Practices	122
• Balancing rewards and values	123
Sub-chapter 4: Passing on Financial Wisdom	124
• Financial Education for Heirs	124
• Family Financial Meetings	124
• Creating a Financial Legacy Plan	125
Sub-chapter 5: Reflections on an Abundant Lifestyle	126
• Appreciation Practices	126
• Reviewing a Life Well-Lived	127
• Preparing for the Next Generation	127
CONCLUSION	**129**
• Reflect on Financial Mastery	129
• Call to Action	130
• Continuous Learning	131
• Financial Freedom Celebration	131

INTRODUCTION

In an age when financial literacy is increasingly regarded as a critical ability, Finance Unleashed shines as a beacon of empowerment and enlightenment. It is more than a set of concepts or tools; it is a paradigm change that allows people to take charge of their financial lives and attain unprecedented levels of wealth and security.

At its heart, Finance Unleashed is about release. It is about breaking free from the limits of traditional financial thinking and adopting a more dynamic and comprehensive approach to wealth management. It's about understanding that finance is more than just making money; it's about making the most of the resources at our disposal, maximizing our financial decisions, and, ultimately, living life on our own terms.

Imagine a future free of financial stress, where everyone possesses the knowledge and abilities to confidently and clearly navigate the intricacies of the financial landscape. This is the world that Finance Unleashed aims to create.

But what exactly is Finance Unleashed and how does it differ from traditional financial advice?

At its core, Finance Unleashed is about empowerment via education. It is about providing people with the knowledge and tools they need to make sound financial decisions, whether they are investing in the stock market, managing debt, or saving for retirement. However, it is more than just information; it is about fostering an attitude of abundance and opportunity, in which financial success is viewed as an attainable reality for anybody willing to work hard.

Furthermore, Finance Unleashed highlights the interconnection of all facets of our financial lives. It recognizes that our financial well-being is impacted by a variety of factors other than our investment returns or savings rate, such as our spending habits, career choices, and even our money attitude. Finance Unleashed is a holistic approach to finance, allowing individuals to optimize all aspects of their financial lives, resulting in more wealth and fulfillment.

In the next pages, we will go deeply into the ideas of Finance Unleashed, including investing methods, budgeting tactics, and wealth-building principles. More than that, we'll look at the mentality shift needed to really unleash the power of finance in our lives—a move that challenges us to challenge common knowledge, examine our assumptions, and embrace the possibilities that lie beyond the limitations of standard financial thinking.

Chapter 1: Understanding the Financial Mindset

Sub-chapter 1: The Influence of Mindset

- **Shift in perspective**

In the field of money, mentality is critical to deciding success. The way one thinks about money, wealth, and financial management can have a substantial impact on their financial outcomes. One of the most influential ideas in this area is to have a growth mentality. A growth mindset, coined by psychologist Carol Dweck, is the concept that one's abilities and intelligence can be developed with devotion and hard work. This perspective stands in stark contrast to the fixed mindset, which holds that abilities are innate and immutable.

Importance of a Growth Mindset in Finance
Adopting a growth mentality in financial affairs can provide several rewards. It allows people to see failures as chances for learning and growth rather than as insurmountable barriers. Those with a growth mindset are more likely to take risks, persevere in the face of adversity, and seek out possibilities for personal development. In terms of personal money,

this approach enables people to continually educate themselves, adapt to changing circumstances, and pursue long-term financial goals with tenacity and commitment.

- ## Case Studies

1-Warren Buffett: Warren Buffett, widely recognized as one of the greatest investors of all time, attributes much of his success to his thinking. Buffett strongly believes in the value of constant learning and progress. Throughout his career, he has highlighted the value of patience, discipline, and a long-term perspective while investing. Despite multiple losses and market downturns, Buffett's growth attitude has allowed him to remain consistent in his investment strategy and finally achieve tremendous financial success.

2) **Oprah Winfrey**
Oprah Winfrey, a media magnate and philanthropist, is another person who has used a growth mentality to attain financial success. Despite enduring severe adversity in her early life, such as poverty and abuse, Winfrey was determined to make a better future for herself. She developed a multibillion-dollar media empire through hard work, determination, and unwavering dedication to her goals. Winfrey's biography demonstrates the transforming potential of

a growth-oriented mindset for overcoming challenges and achieving financial success.

- **Action Steps:**

"Let's turn inspiration into action. Here are some practical measures for cultivating a growth-oriented financial mindset:

1- Daily Affirmations: Start each day with positive affirmations about your financial goals. Affirmations act as a reminder of your capacity for progress and help to establish a resilient mindset.

2- Learning Mindset: Adopt the mindset of a constant learner. Actively pursue financial education, whether through books, podcasts, or classes. The more you know, the better prepared you are to confront financial issues.

3- Visualize prosperity: Every day, take time to visualize your financial prosperity. Consider attaining your goals, conquering challenges, and enjoying the emotions that come with financial success. Visualization reinforces the sense that achievement is not just conceivable but unavoidable.

4- Challenge Negative beliefs: Actively question and rephrase negative beliefs regarding money. When confronted with ideas of shortage or skepticism, actively replace them with thoughts of abundance and possibility.

5- Celebrate Progress: Recognize and celebrate your financial successes, no matter how modest. Celebrations promote positive actions and serve to strengthen the sense that progress is being made.

Remember that these action steps are more than simply jobs; they are the foundation for a mindset that will propel you to financial mastery. By incorporating these habits into your daily life, you are not only changing your thinking but also actively shaping your financial future.

Sub-chapter 2: Overcome Financial Limiting Beliefs

- ### Identifying beliefs

Many people have restrictive attitudes about money that impede their financial progress. These ideas are frequently deeply embedded and can emerge in a variety of ways, including:
"Money is the root of all evil."
"I'll never be wealthy."
"I'm not smart enough to manage my finances."

- ### Debunking Myths

1- Money is the root of evil:Contrary to popular beliefs, money is neither good nor bad. It is merely a tool that may be used in both positive and negative ways. By reframing this notion, people can see how money can be a positive influence in their lives and the lives of others.

2- I'll Never Be Wealthy: This idea is typically the result of a stuck mindset and a lack of faith in one's capacity to attain financial success. However, countless people from various backgrounds have become wealthy through hard work, dedication, and intelligent financial planning. Individuals who challenge this assumption and focus on tangible activities to improve their financial status boost their chances of becoming wealthy.

3- I am not smart enough to manage my finances. Financial management is a talent that can be learned and improved with time. While some people may be intimidated by financial concepts at first, with determination and education, they may develop the knowledge and confidence they need to handle their money successfully. Individuals who seek resources such as books, courses, and expert help can overcome this limiting belief and regain control of their financial future.

- **Reprogramming Strategies**

1. Cognitive restructuring: Examine the evidence and examine alternate points of view to challenge negative financial beliefs. Replace limiting thoughts with empowering affirmations that are consistent with your financial goals and objectives.

2. Visualization: Visualize yourself achieving financial success and the beneficial impact it will have on your lifestyle. Visualizing your objectives and aspirations on a daily basis might help to reinforce positive thoughts and drive you to take action to achieve them.

3. Affirmations: Create and repeat affirmations that promote a growth attitude on a daily basis. In other words, "I am capable of achieving financial success" as well as "I am committed to learning and growing my wealth."

4. Education: Invest in your financial knowledge by reading books, attending seminars, and obtaining guidance from financial professionals. The more you learn about personal finance, the more confident and equipped you will be to manage your money successfully.

5. Accountability: Hold yourself accountable for questioning and revising limiting assumptions about money. Surround yourself with helpful people who can inspire you and hold you accountable for your financial goals.

Subchapter 3: Developing a Wealth Mindset

- **Understanding Wealth: Redefining Beyond Monetary Aspect**

Wealth is often connected with monetary riches, although it refers to much more than that. True wealth encompasses many aspects of life, such as physical health, mental well-being, rewarding relationships, personal development, and a sense of purpose. When redefining wealth, it is critical to shift away from a solely materialistic perspective and toward a holistic one that takes into account overall pleasure and contentment.

Individuals might begin redefining wealth by establishing their primary values and priorities. This entails focusing on what is important to them beyond material belongings and money. It could include things like good health, meaningful relationships, personal development, and contributing to society. Individuals who recognize and appreciate these non-monetary components of prosperity might live a more balanced and meaningful life.

Furthermore, comprehending wealth necessitates recognizing the abundance attitude versus the scarcity perspective. An abundance mindset sees opportunities and possibilities everywhere, which encourages thankfulness and optimism. A scarcity mindset, on the other hand, concentrates on restrictions and lacks, which causes dread, anxiety, and the sense that there is never enough. Cultivating an abundant mindset is essential for developing a wealth mindset because it promotes resourcefulness, resilience, and creativity in achieving financial goals.

- **Visualization Techniques**

A wealth mindset can be developed, and financial success can be manifested with the use of visualization. People can raise their chances of reaching their financial goals by directing their thoughts, feelings, and behaviors toward them and visualizing their intended results.

This is a manual for efficient visualization methods:

1- Set clear goals: First, establish SMART (specific, measurable, attainable, relevant, and time-bound) financial objectives. When it comes to visualizing goals such as saving a specific amount of money, paying off debt, or earning passive income, the secret to success is clarity.

2- Create a Vision Board: Gather photos, quotations, and symbols that symbolize your financial goals and desires. Arrange them on a vision board and keep them in a conspicuous position where you can regularly visualize and reinforce your goals.

3- Practice Daily Visualization: Set aside time each day to perform visualization exercises. Close your eyes, relax your mind and body, and imagine yourself attaining your financial goals in vivid detail. Consider the feelings, sensations, and experiences related to your success.

4- Use Affirmations: Combine visualization with positive affirmations that strengthen your belief in reaching financial success. Repeat affirmations like "I am financially abundant" or "money flows effortlessly into my life" to boost your confidence and conviction in your goals.

5- Feel gratitude: Develop a sense of thankfulness for your current financial condition and the wealth around you. Expressing appreciation boosts pleasant feelings and draws additional rewards into your life.

6- Stay Consistent: Consistency is essential for good visualization. Make it a daily habit, even while facing obstacles or disappointments. Believe in the process, and stick to your financial goals.

Individuals who incorporate these visualization techniques into their everyday routines can use the power of their subconscious mind to materialize financial success and cultivate a wealth-oriented mindset.

- **Implementing Wealth Habits**

Cultivating a wealth-oriented mindset entails developing practical habits and behaviors that are conducive to financial success.

Here are some actionable habits you can implement

1- Financial Education: Invest in ongoing education about personal finance, investing, and wealth-building tactics. Read books, attend seminars, and seek advice from financial professionals to improve your financial literacy and make better judgments.

2- Budgeting and Saving: Make a budget and allocate funds to savings, investments, and necessary expenses. Monitor your spending habits to uncover areas where you might cut expenditures and save more effectively. Set aside a percentage of your income for savings and emergencies to create a financial safety net.

3- Goal Setting: Set specific, attainable financial goals and divide them into smaller milestones. Create a plan of action that outlines specific steps for achieving each goal, and track your progress regularly. Celebrate your accomplishments along the way to stay motivated and focused.

4- Mindful Spending: To practice mindful spending, discriminate between needs and wants. Prioritize purchases that are consistent with your values and long-term goals, while limiting impulse spending and unnecessary expenses. Develop financial discipline and avoid spending more than you can afford.

5- Investing for the Future: Take sensible risks by investing in assets with the potential for long-term gains, such as stocks, real estate, or retirement funds. Diversify your investing portfolio to reduce risks while increasing potential for development. Start investing early to get the benefits of compound interest.

6- Networking and Mentorship: Surround yourself with people who inspire and motivate you to be financially successful. Create a network of like-minded peers, mentors, and advisers who can offer advice, support, and invaluable insights into wealth-building tactics.

7- Positive Mindset and Resilience: Develop a positive attitude that sees setbacks as opportunities for growth and learning. Develop resilience in the face of setbacks and disappointments, viewing them as transitory roadblocks on the route to achievement.Maintain your focus on your goals and believe in your abilities to overcome hurdles and attain financial prosperity.

By persistently practicing these money habits, individuals may gradually shift their thinking and actions to fit with their financial goals, opening the road for long-term prosperity and fulfillment.

Sub-chapter 4: Embracing Risk and Opportunity

• Risk Perception

Risk perception is an individual's subjective appraisal of the probability and implications of uncertain events. Cognitive biases, emotions, previous experiences, and cultural influences all have an impact on the psychology of risk aversion.Understanding these dynamics is critical for successful risk management and making sound financial decisions.

1- Cognitive Biases: Humans are susceptible to cognitive biases, which affect rational decision-making. Common biases like loss aversion, anchoring, and confirmation bias can cause people to exaggerate dangers or underestimate possibilities, limiting their capacity to take prudent risks.

2- Emotions: Emotions play an important role in risk perception, often clouding judgment and exacerbating worries about prospective losses. Fear, greed, and overconfidence can skew risk evaluations, leading to rash or foolish financial decisions.

3- Past Experiences: Previous successes and failures can influence one's risk assessment. Positive experiences may encourage a willingness to accept risks, but negative experiences might build dread and resistance to uncertainty.

4- Cultural Influences: Society's expectations and cultural norms have an impact on how people perceive danger. While cultures that promote entrepreneurship and innovation may be more inclined towards risk-taking behavior, cultures that place a greater priority on stability and security may also display higher degrees of risk aversion.

Through an understanding of the psychological elements that underlie risk perception, people can lessen the influence of emotions and biases on their decision-making, leading to more logical and knowledgeable choices when managing financial risks.

- **Balancing Risks**

Balancing risks means weighing the prospective benefits against the likelihood and severity of negative events.

Here are some techniques to effectively manage financial risks:

1- Diversification: Diversification is spreading assets across asset classes, industries, and geographic locations to mitigate the effects of individual market swings. Diversification helps to lessen the specific risks associated with a single investment or sector.

2- Risk Assessment: Conduct extensive risk assessments by examining aspects such as volatility, liquidity, and the correlation between investments. Before committing funds to any investment opportunity, consider the potential downside risks and rewards.

3- Asset Allocation: Distribute assets depending on individual risk tolerance, investment objectives, and time frame. Adjust asset allocation over time to provide a balanced portfolio that responds to changing market conditions and personal circumstances.

4- Risk management: Implement risk management measures like stop-loss orders, hedging techniques, and portfolio rebalancing to reduce downside risks and protect capital amid market volatility.

5- Continuous Monitoring: Monitor investment portfolios and financial markets regularly to discover developing dangers and opportunities. Stay current on macroeconomic trends, geopolitical events, and industry-specific developments that may affect investment performance.

6- Long-Term Perspective: When weighing financial risks and benefits, keep the big picture in mind. Focus on the fundamentals of investing and resist the need to respond rashly to short-term market swings.

Individuals who incorporate these risk management measures into their investment strategy can effectively balance risks and improve their chances of long-term financial development and stability.

- ## Seizing Opportunities

It's frequently necessary to be willing to take measured chances and move beyond one's comfort zone to seize possibilities. Taking a risk has the potential to be uncertain and costly, but it can also result in large financial rewards.

This is the relationship between taking risks and financial success

1- Higher Return Potential: In the world of finance, there is an innate relationship between risk and return, with higher risk levels generally translating into the possibility of larger returns. People can gradually raise their potential for financial rewards by accepting risk and pursuing investment opportunities with favorable risk-return profiles.

2- Innovation and Entrepreneurship: The two disciplines benefit greatly from taking risks. Despite the uncertainty, successful inventors and businesspeople aren't afraid to disrupt the status quo, take calculated chances, and go for fresh opportunities. Individuals can open up new opportunities for wealth growth by taking on risks.

3- Learning and Growth: By pushing people to take on obstacles, draw lessons from their experiences, and adjust to changing conditions, risk-taking promotes both professional and personal growth. Accepting risk fosters adaptability, resourcefulness, and a growth mentality—all necessary for securing financial success in fast-paced, cutthroat markets.

4- Opportunity Cost: Missed chances and slow growth may arise from completely avoiding risk. People can achieve a balance between risk aversion and risk-taking behavior by carefully weighing the benefits and hazards. This allows them to make the best financial decisions possible, maximizing long-term gains while reducing prospective losses.

In the end, taking on risks is essential to grabbing hold of chances and realizing the full potential of wealth and financial progress. People can put themselves in a position to benefit from risk by comprehending how risk is perceived, putting effective risk management techniques into practice, and accepting measured risk-taking behavior.

Sub-chapter 5: Mastering the Art of Patience

• Delayed Gratification

Delayed gratification is the ability to forego current rewards in favor of larger rewards in the future. In the context of financial planning, it entails making sacrifices and showing restraint in spending or investing to attain long-term financial objectives.

Benefits of Delayed Gratification
1- Wealth Accumulation: By deferring immediate consumption and instead saving or investing money, people can build wealth over time through compound interest and capital appreciation.

2- Financial Security: By delaying gratification, people can save emergency money, pay off debts, and protect their financial future from unanticipated situations.

3- Long-Term Goal Achievement: Prioritizing long-term goals such as retirement savings, homeownership, or education money can lead to greater future pleasure and contentment.

4- Improved Decision-Making: Delayed gratification promotes discipline and self-control, resulting in better financial decisions and less impulsivity.

- **Long-Term Vision: Stories of Success Through Patience**

Warren Buffett

Warren Buffett, called the "Oracle of Omaha," is well known for his long-term investment strategy and incredible patience. Despite market instability and economic downturns, Buffett stayed committed to value investing, holding onto investments for decades. His patience and dedication have paid off handsomely, and he is now one of the most successful investors of all time.

Jeff Bezos

Jeff Bezos, the founder of Amazon, shows the importance of patience and tenacity in business. Bezos started Amazon in 1994 and spent years transforming the company from a small online bookshop to the e-commerce empire.

- **Practical Patience Techniques: Cultivating Patience In Financial Endeavors**

1. Set clear goals: Set defined, achievable financial goals with realistic dates. Break down larger goals into smaller milestones and track your progress regularly. Having a clear roadmap might help you stay focused and motivated over time.

2. Practice mindfulness: Incorporate mindfulness practices like meditation, deep breathing, and visualization into your daily routine. Mindfulness can help you reduce stress, develop self-awareness, and be more patient when making financial decisions.

3. Create a long-term investment strategy: Create a diverse investment portfolio that is in line with your long-term financial objectives and risk tolerance. Avoid the temptation to seek short-term gains or react rashly to market volatility. Stick to your investment approach and believe in the power of compounding over time.

4. Automate savings and investments: Create automatic transfers from your paycheck or bank account to savings or investing accounts. Automating your donations eliminates the need for willpower and ensures continuous progress toward your financial goals.

5. Seek support and accountability: Enlist the help of a financial advisor, mentor, or accountability partner to guide, inspire, and hold you accountable on your financial journey. Having someone to discuss your objectives and progress with will help you stay inspired and accountable to your long-term vision.

6. Practice gratitude: Cultivate a grateful attitude toward your accomplishments and the resources at your disposal. Celebrate minor triumphs along the road and celebrate the joys in your life, encouraging a positive outlook and strengthening your commitment to financial endeavors.

Chapter 2: Strategic Savings and Spending

Sub-Chapter 1: The Saving Mindset

- **Importance of Savings**

Saving is the foundation of financial success, giving people the ability to achieve their goals, withstand financial storms, and accumulate wealth over time. Individuals who prioritize saving can lay a solid foundation for their financial future.

1- Financial Security

Savings offer financial security by covering unexpected bills or emergencies. Savings allow individuals to meet necessities without incurring high-interest debt or exhausting other financial resources.

2- Goal Achievement

Saving allows people to achieve their financial goals, such as buying a house, starting a business, or retiring comfortably. Individuals can make progress toward their goals and make their aspirations a reality by saving money regularly.

3- Wealth Accumulation

Saving is the first step toward money accumulation. Individuals who continuously save and invest money might take advantage of compound interest to enhance their wealth over time. Over time, even tiny contributions might add up to considerable sums.

- **Automated Saving**

Ensuring consistency and discipline in saving habits can be effectively achieved by automating the savings process. People can prioritize saving without constant effort or decision-making by setting up automated transfers.

1- Direct Deposit: One of the easiest ways to automate savings is to directly deposit a portion of each paycheck into a savings account. Savings can become a priority for people if they set aside a percentage of their salary for savings before it's even received.

2- Transitions by Autonomy: Automating regular transfers of funds from a checking account to a savings account is another efficient way to automate savings. Without the need for human intervention, this "set it and forget it" strategy guarantees that savings contributions happen regularly.

3- Round-Up Software: The difference is transferred into a savings or investment account by round-up applications, which connect to users' bank accounts and automatically round up each transaction to the nearest dollar. Saving money is made simple and doesn't even require conscious effort by users.

• Emergency Funds: Beyond Expenses and Income

An essential part of financial planning is emergency savings, which act as a safety net against unforeseen costs and disruptions. People can shield themselves from financial hardships and preserve stability in trying times by creating and keeping an emergency fund.

1- The Need for Emergency Money

Emergency savings are necessary to pay for unforeseen costs like hospital bills, auto repairs, or job losses. In times of disaster, having an emergency fund in place can keep people from going into debt or emptying their savings accounts.

2- Creating a Fund for Emergencies

People should prioritize fund contributions and set savings targets to accumulate an emergency fund. Aim to save three to six months' worth of living expenses to begin with, and then progressively increase the amount of the fund over time.

3- Sustaining the Reserve

After the emergency fund is established, it must be routinely reviewed and replenished to take changing income or cost trends into consideration. Even in times of economic stability, prioritize payments to the fund and treat it as a non-negotiable expense.

Sub-chapter 2: Creating a Budget That Works

- ## Holistic Budgeting

Holistic budgeting is more than just recording costs and income; it takes into account all areas of one's financial life to construct a comprehensive budget that is consistent with one's goals and values.

1- Goal-oriented budgeting

Rather than focusing merely on income and expenses, goal-oriented budgeting entails establishing specific financial objectives and allocating resources accordingly. This method ensures that every dollar serves a purpose and contributes to the targeted goals.

2- Savings and investments

Savings and investments are prioritized in holistic budgeting as essential components of financial planning. Individuals contribute a percentage of their income to savings accounts, retirement plans, and other investment vehicles to accumulate wealth over time.

3- Debt Management

Debt management is another key component of holistic budgeting. Individuals set aside money to pay off debts, such as credit card bills, school loans, or mortgages, to reduce interest expenses and increase financial stability.

- **Expense Tracking: Tools and Strategy**

Effective expense tracking is critical for analyzing spending trends, identifying areas for improvement, and adhering to financial goals.

Here are some tools and ideas for properly tracking your expenses:

1- Budgeting Applications and Software

Budgeting tools and software, such as Mint, YNAB (You Need a Budget), and Personal Capital, automate expense tracking, categorize spending, and provide information about financial patterns. These apps provide simplicity and accessibility to consumers wishing to streamline their budgeting process.

2- Manual Tracking Methods

For individuals who prefer a more hands-on approach, manual tracking methods such as spreadsheets, notes, or envelopes can be useful. Individuals can use these approaches to manually organize receipts, log expenses, and manage spending, giving them more control and flexibility.

3- Budget Adjustments:

A good budget is versatile and responsive to changing circumstances and priorities. Here's how people can make dynamic changes to their budget:

4- Regular Reviews

Regular budget reviews, such as monthly or quarterly, enable personnel to analyze progress, identify areas for improvement, and make required modifications. This proactive strategy guarantees that the budget remains in line with current financial objectives and circumstances.

5- Prioritizing spending

When resources are scarce, prioritizing spending becomes critical. Individuals should allocate resources based on their values and objectives, focusing on what provides them the most joy and fulfillment while reducing unnecessary expenses.

6- Emergency adjustments

Having provisions in place for unforeseen events, such as job loss or medical emergency, promotes financial stability and resilience. Individuals should be prepared to make emergency budget modifications, such as lowering discretionary spending or tapping into emergency funds, to deal with unexpected obstacles.

Subchapter 3: Mindful Spending

- **Conscious Consumption**

Conscious consumption is the conscious and mindful examination of purchases to minimize waste while prioritizing sustainable and ethical products and services. Adopting mindful spending habits entails becoming more conscious of the effects of our purchasing decisions on ourselves, others, and the environment.

Practicing conscientious consumption requires several fundamental principles:

1- Awareness: Gaining an understanding of where your money goes and how it relates to your ideals. This entails frequently assessing your spending patterns and determining if each purchase is required or adds value to your life.

2- Sustainability: selecting goods and services with the least possible negative effects on the environment. This could be avoiding single-use plastics, choosing reusable or environmentally friendly alternatives, and supporting businesses that follow sustainable business practices.

3- Ethics: Think about the moral consequences of your purchases, including how fair trade methods, worker treatment, and your support of socially conscious companies are handled.

4- Quality above quantity: Putting quality above quantity might result in longer-lasting, more valuable purchases that are ultimately more gratifying. This change in perspective can discourage impulsive purchases and promote spending on long-lasting, premium goods.

Through the practice of conscious consumption, people can cultivate a stronger sense of fulfillment and purpose in their purchasing habits, as well as positively impact society and the environment.

- **Value-Based Spending**

Aligning your financial decisions with your priorities and fundamental values is known as value-based spending. You can use your resources more wisely and purposefully if you know what's most important to you—be it community, education, health, or personal development.

The following are steps to implement value-based spending

1- Determine Your Values: Consider the things in life that are most important to you. These could be more general ideals like social justice, sustainability, or philanthropy, or they could be more intimate values like family, health, or education.

2- Spending Prioritization: After determining your values, order your expenditures following those priorities. Set aside more of your budget for costs that support your top priorities, and think about reducing costs that don't support your principles.

3- Establish Goals: Whether it's saving for a child's education, making experience investments, or contributing to charitable causes, establish clear financial goals that are consistent with your values. Having specific goals will help you stay focused on what is important and will influence your spending selections.

4- Regularly Evaluate: Make sure your expenditure is in line with your objectives and beliefs by reviewing it regularly. Make any necessary adjustments to your budget and be open to changing it to better represent your changing objectives.

People can live more meaningful and purposeful lives and find more happiness and significance in their financial decisions when they connect their spending with their own values.

- ## Cutting superfluous expenses

Reducing wasteful spending is crucial for strengthening financial stability and releasing funds for worthwhile endeavors.

The following useful advice can be used to recognize and cut back on wasteful spending:

1- Monitor Your Expenses: For a month, keep tabs on every penny you spend to spot trends and potential areas of overspending. Sort spending into categories and pinpoint areas that need improvement by using spreadsheets or budgeting tools.

2- Question Every Purchase: Before making any purchases, consider whether they are in line with your priorities and values. Think about whether you need the good or service, or whether there are less expensive options.

3- Put Needs Before Wants: Make a distinction between spending on necessities (needs) and luxuries (wants). Give priority to necessities like food, shelter, and medical care, and cut back on discretionary spending on non-essentials.

4- Shop with Mindfulness: By being conscious when you shop, you can prevent impulsive purchases. Before you visit the store, make a list and follow it to prevent making unneeded purchases. When buying something, weigh the costs and determine whether you need it.

5- Smart Shopper: Seek out chances to negotiate for a better deal or a lower price. As an alternative to buying new, think about renting or buying used goods. To save money on routine expenses, make use of discounts and reward programs.

6- Examine subscriptions and memberships: To ascertain whether you are receiving value from your subscriptions and memberships, periodically review them. To save money, cancel any memberships or subscriptions that you are no longer using.

7- Automate Savings: Set up automatic transfers to savings or investing accounts to guarantee that you continuously save for future goals. Pay yourself first by setting aside a percentage of your salary before paying for other expenses.

Individuals can use these tactics to discover and decrease wasteful costs, freeing up money for more important activities and long-term financial goals. Mindful spending not only increases financial well-being but also promotes a stronger sense of fulfillment and purpose in life.

Sub-chapter 4: Power of Compounding

- **Compounding**

Compound interest is the process of adding interest to both the starting principal and the accumulated interest from prior periods, resulting in an exponential increase over time. Unlike simple interest, which only accrues on the initial principle, compound interest increases investment growth, resulting in significant long-term returns.

The compound interest formula is as follows: A = P x (1 + r/nn).
Where:
A represents the future worth of the investment or loan, including interest.
P = the initial investment amount.
r represents the annual interest rate (in decimal).
n is the number of times interest is compounded per year.
The term "t" refers to the duration of the investment in years.
Compound interest has a huge impact since it allows even small returns to rise dramatically over time. By reinvesting earnings and allowing them to compound over time, investors can leverage the power of compounding to accumulate significant wealth.

- **Investing strategy**

The following investment vehicles allow people to make use of compounding's power

1- Stocks and Equities: Buying stocks gives investors a chance to be part of a company's growth and has the potential to yield large returns over time. The compounding of returns is facilitated by both capital appreciation and dividends.

2-Bonds: Fixed-income instruments with a regular interest rate are available; these can be reinvested to generate compound returns. Compared to stocks, bonds offer a more cautious investing alternative with less volatility and possibly lower returns.

3- Mutual funds and exchange-traded funds (ETFs): These investment vehicles aggregate investors' capital to allocate it among a diverse array of assets, thereby offering exposure to a broad spectrum of securities. Compounding returns are aided by capital gains and reinvested dividends.

4- Retirement funds: Long-term compound growth prospects are provided by tax-advantaged retirement funds like 401(k)s and IRAs. Frequently, contributions are tax-deductible, and profits accumulate tax-free or tax-deferred until they are withdrawn.

- ### Time as a partner

Time is an important aspect of realizing the potential of compounding. The longer the investing horizon, the greater the likelihood of exponential development. Starting early allows investors to benefit from longer compounding periods, which increases the impact of gains over time.

Individuals who prioritize early investing and remain dedicated to a long-term strategy can maximize compounding rewards and accumulate significant wealth over time. Time is undoubtedly the most powerful ally on the path to financial freedom and wealth building.

Sub-chapter 5: Advanced Savings and Investing Techniques

- ### Tax-Efficient Strategies

Tax-efficient solutions are critical for reducing tax bills and increasing after-tax earnings. The key tax-efficient solutions include tax-advantaged accounts:

1- Use tax-advantaged accounts like 401(k), IRAs, and Health Savings Accounts (HSAs) to defer or avoid paying taxes on contributions and investment earnings.

2- Tax-Loss Harvesting: To offset capital gains, sell losing investments to recover losses that can be used to lower taxable income.

3- Asset Allocation: To maximize tax efficiency, strategically distribute assets between taxable and tax-advantaged accounts. Put tax-inefficient investments in tax-advantaged accounts and tax-efficient investments in taxable accounts.

4- Roth Conversions: Consider converting traditional retirement account assets to Roth funds to take advantage of tax-free withdrawals in retirement.

- **Diversification**

Diversification is a risk management approach in which investments are distributed over several asset classes, industries, and geographic locations to reduce portfolio volatility and mitigate the impact of individual security risks.

The advantages of diversification include
1- Risk Reduction: Diversification reduces the impact of adverse occurrences on individual investments by spreading risk across a wider variety of assets.
2- Enhanced Returns: By capitalizing on the performance of several asset classes, a well-diversified portfolio has the potential to deliver more consistent long-term returns.
3- Smoothing Volatility: Diversification helps reduce portfolio volatility, giving investors a more consistent investment experience.

- **Leveraging Financial Instruments**

Sophisticated instruments for investing and saving allow for the management of risk and the optimization of rewards. Among them are:
1- Derivatives: By using leverage, investors can increase portfolio returns, speculate on market fluctuations, and hedge against risk by using derivative products like options, futures, and swaps.

2- Margin Trading: By borrowing money from a broker to buy assets, investors can increase their potential returns while also taking on more risk.

3- Alternative Investments: Although they can have higher minimum investment requirements and involve more complexity and risk, alternative investments like real estate, hedge funds, and private equity can provide benefits to diversification and the possibility of increased returns.

Chapter 3: Maximizing Income Streams

Sub-chapter 1: Beyond 9–5

- ### Side Hustles

Side hustles are part-time or freelance jobs that people do in addition to their full-time jobs to earn more money and have more flexibility.

Popular side hustles include

1- Freelancing Services: Provide talents and knowledge in writing, graphic design, programming, and virtual help through sites such as Upwork, Fiverr, or TaskRabbit.

2- E-commerce: E-commerce is the practice of selling products online using platforms such as Etsy, eBay, or Shopify, whether through handmade goods, dropshipping, or retail arbitrage.

3- Gig Economy Jobs: delivering meals with DoorDash or Uber Eats, driving for rideshare services like Uber or Lyft, or finishing jobs on websites like TaskRabbit or Gigwalk.

4- Consulting: Consulting is the practice of offering people and companies advice in fields including business, marketing, finance, and technology.

4- Tutoring and Teaching: Providing academic tutoring, music lessons, language training, and online courses, among other tutoring services.

- **Freelancing Opportunities**

Freelancing allows people to work on a project basis for a variety of clients, typically remotely.

Popular freelancer platforms include:

1- Upwork: A top platform for freelancers in a variety of industries, connecting businesses with talented experts for projects ranging from short-term engagements to long-term contracts.

2- Freelancers: Similar to Upwork, offer a diverse range of freelance opportunities in writing, design, programming, and marketing.

3- Fiverr: Fiverr is a platform where independent contractors can list their services in various categories, or "gigs," with a $5 minimum charge. It is renowned for providing a wide range of expert and innovative services.

4- Toptal: Toptal is an organization that connects companies with the best independent contractors in industries including project management, design, finance, and software development.

5- Guru: This platform supports a variety of freelancing abilities, such as writing, design, marketing, and administrative assistance.

- **Passive Income Streams**

Making money with little continuous work or direct involvement is known as passive income streams.

A few examples are:

1- Investing: Investing in stocks or funds that pay monthly dividends to shareholders based on business profits is known as dividend investing.

2- Royalties: receiving payments from the use or sale of intellectual property, such as books, music, artwork, or patents.

3- Rental Income: Making money by renting out space to tenants on rental properties, whether they are residential or commercial.

4- Affiliate marketing: Affiliate marketing is the practice of promoting goods or services through affiliate links in order to receive a commission for any sales that result from your referral.

Sub-chapter 2: Negotiation Mastery

- **Wage Negotiation**

To maximize earning potential and advance in one's profession, one must negotiate a higher wage.

Important techniques for negotiating pay include

1- Research: To provide a starting point for negotiations, look into local compensation ranges and industry norms for roles that are comparable to yours.

2- Emphasize Value: To prove your worth and get paid more, highlight your achievements, talents, and contributions to the company.

3- Be Ready to Walk Away: If the offered salary does not satisfy your needs or fit with market rates, be prepared to end the negotiation.

4- Discuss advantages: In addition to pay, talk about negotiating other advantages like stock options, bonuses, flexible work schedules, or chances for professional growth.

- **Contract Negotiation**

For business professionals, entrepreneurs, and freelancers alike, contract negotiation is an essential skill.

Important points for effective contract negotiations consist of:

1- Recognize Terms: Carefully go over the terms and conditions of the agreement, taking note of important phrases including the deliverables, payment terms, scope of work, and termination clauses.

2- Define Expectations: To guarantee agreement on project scope, schedules, and deliverables, express expectations to the customer or counterparty clearly and concisely.

3- Negotiate scope changes: Be ready to bargain for modifications to the project's parameters or extra services the client requests, making sure that any extra time or resources needed are fairly compensated.

4- Seek legal assistance: To make sure that your interests are sufficiently safeguarded and that the contract is legally enforceable, you should think about obtaining legal assistance for complex or high-value agreements.

- ## Negotiation Psychology

Understanding the psychology of negotiating might offer you a competitive advantage in getting positive results.

The key principles include

1- Empathy: Understanding the other party's viewpoints and motives to establish rapport and create collaboration during negotiations.

2- Assertiveness: Clearly express your wants and preferences while remaining open to compromise and seeking mutually beneficial solutions.

3- Anchoring: Use anchoring strategies to provide a good starting point for negotiations by influencing the opposing party's perception of value and prospective results.

4- Emotional Intelligence: Recognize and control your own and the other party's emotions to continue healthy discussions and avoid problems during negotiations.

Sub-chapter 3: Entrepreneurial Ventures

- **Identifying Opportunities**

Identifying sustainable business prospects takes ingenuity, market research, and a thorough understanding of consumer needs.

Key steps include:

1- Market Research: Conduct extensive market research to uncover trends, gaps, and unmet needs in your target market. Analyze competition and client preferences to identify potential opportunities.

2- Problem-Solving: Look for challenges or pain points that consumers or businesses face and investigate inventive ways to successfully address them.

3- Expertise and Passion: Think about going after business ventures that complement your skills, interests, and passions. Your chances of success and fulfillment might rise by making the most of your knowledge and abilities.

4- Customer validation: Get input on company concepts from prospective clients via questionnaires, interviews, or prototype testing. Verify whether the suggested good or service is actually in demand.

- **Startup Strategies**

A successful startup needs to be carefully planned, executed, and flexible to grow. Crucial tactics consist of...

1- Making a Business Plan: Draft a thorough business plan that outlines the target market, value proposition, revenue model, growth strategy, and objectives of the organization.

2- Putting Together a Great Team: Assemble a bright, diverse group of people who have complementary abilities and a common goal for the company's success.

3- Minimal viable product (MVP): Create a prototype or minimally viable product to test the market and get input from early users. Refine the product or service by iterating according to customer input.

4- Marketing and Branding: To draw clients and set the startup apart from rivals, create a compelling brand identity and marketing plan. To efficiently contact target audiences, make use of social media, content marketing, and digital marketing channels.

5- Scaling Operations: As the company develops, concentrate on growing into new markets or clientele segments, streamlining procedures, and scaling operations. Invest in personnel, infrastructure, and technology to support expansion while upholding standards of quality and client satisfaction.

- ## Risk Management in Entrepreneurship

Risks are a natural part of being an entrepreneur, but good risk management can reduce possible hazards and increase success rates.

Important approaches to risk management consist of:

1- Diversification: To reduce dependence on any one revenue stream, market segment, or client base, diversify your product offerings, customer bases, and revenue streams.

2- Financial Planning: To weather unforeseen costs, economic downturns, or cash flow issues, keep sufficient financial reserves and backup plans.

3- Legal and Regulatory Compliance: To guarantee compliance and reduce legal risks, keep up with pertinent laws, rules, and industry standards. Seek advice from financial and legal professionals as needed.

4- Insurance Coverage: To guard against liabilities, property damage, and other unanticipated events that could cause operations to be disrupted, think about getting the right insurance coverage.

5- Constant Risk Assessment and Monitoring: Evaluate and track the business's risks regularly, adjusting strategies and backup plans as necessary to deal with new dangers or opportunities.

Entrepreneurs may better manage obstacles and position their businesses for long-term success and sustainability by proactively identifying and managing risks.

Sub-chapter 4: Investing in yourself

- **Continuous Learning**

Maintaining competitiveness in the quickly changing employment environment of today requires constant learning.

Important tactics for continuing education and developing one's skills consist of:

1- Formal Education: Seek out postgraduate degrees, certificates, or specialized training courses that are pertinent to your sector of work or professional objectives.

2- Online Courses and Resources: Learn on your own time and gain new skills by utilizing flexible online learning platforms like Coursera, Udemy, or LinkedIn Learning.

3- Professional Development Workshops: To stay current on market trends, best practices, and new technology, attend conferences, seminars, workshops, and networking events.

4- Mentoring and coaching: Seek assistance from seasoned experts or mentors who may offer insightful counsel, sound judgment, and career advice drawn from their personal experiences.

- **Professional Networking**

Establishing a strong professional network is essential for advancing one's career, finding employment, and receiving professional assistance.

<u>**Crucial advice for successful networking includes the following:**</u>

1- Attend networking events: To meet professionals and grow your network, and take part in industry conferences, seminars, trade exhibitions, and networking events.

2- Make use of social media: Make connections with coworkers, peers in the business, recruiters, and possible mentors by using sites like LinkedIn. Assemble a professional network and engage in conversations by joining organizations that are pertinent to your industry.

3- Informational Interviews: To gain insight into the career pathways, experiences, and perspectives of professionals in your field of interest, do informational interviews with them. Develop sincere connections and show your appreciation for their guidance and time.

4- Give Back: Whenever possible, offer your network members aid, support, and resources. Networking is a two-way street, and building mutually beneficial relationships is critical to long-term success.

- **Personal Branding**

Developing a distinct personality and reputation that represent your beliefs, knowledge, and career objectives is known as personal branding.

Important components of one's brand comprise:

1- Define your brand: Determine the qualities, interests, and special selling propositions that set you apart from competitors in your industry. Create a captivating narrative for your brand that conveys your goals, values, and story.

2- Online Presence: Use a personal website, a blog, or professional social media sites to build a strong online presence where you can interact with readers, offer insights, and demonstrate your area of expertise.

3- Consistency: Keep your visual identity, communication style, and brand messaging consistent across all platforms and interactions. Being consistent helps you gain credibility and trust from your audience.

4- Networking: Make use of your brand to draw in opportunities such as joint ventures, employment offers, and speaking engagements. Make use of your network to broaden your audience and strengthen your brand.

5- Continuous Improvement: Adjust and improve your brand on an ongoing basis in response to market developments, customer feedback, and changing professional objectives.

Invest in your professional growth and skill improvement to build your brand and maintain relevance in your industry. Through the implementation of strategies such as investing in ongoing education, establishing a robust professional network, and crafting a compelling personal brand, individuals can optimize their career options, draw in profitable opportunities, and attain sustained success and satisfaction.

Sub-Chapter 5: Achieving Financial Independence

- ### FIRE Movement

The FIRE movement promotes financial independence through active saving, investing, and lifestyle choices, allowing people to retire early and follow their interests without financial restraints.

The key principles of the FIRE movement are:

1- Financial independence is defined as generating enough passive income or investment returns to pay living expenses without relying on traditional employment.

2- Retire Early: Leaving full-time employment at a younger age, usually in one's 40s or even sooner, to pursue personal interests, hobbies, or entrepreneurial enterprises.

3- Economical living: living a minimalist and economical lifestyle to cut costs, build savings, and expedite the path to financial independence.

4- Investment Strategy: To create wealth over time, focus on high savings rates, disciplined investing in low-cost index funds or income-producing assets, and reducing wasteful expenses.

- Calculating the FI Number

The financial independence number, or FI number, is the amount of savings or investment needed to meet living expenditures permanently without requiring further income.

The steps for calculating the FI number are:

1- Estimate annual expenses: Determine your current annual expenses, which include housing, food, transportation, health care, and discretionary spending.

2- Multiply by the safe withdrawal rate: To determine the amount of funds required to pay annual expenses sustainably, use a safe withdrawal rate, which normally ranges between 3% and 4% each year.

3- Modify for Inflation: To keep purchasing power over time, modify your FI figure to reflect inflation and potential spending fluctuations.

4- Factor in Other Income Sources: To reduce your reliance on investment returns, factor in other sources of income when calculating your FI number, such as rental income, pensions, or social security payments.

5- Review and update frequently: To make sure your FI figure is in line with your financial objectives, review and update it regularly, depending on changes in spending, investment performance, and life circumstances.

Chapter 4: Mastering Investment Strategies

Sub-chapter 1: Risk-Adjusted Returns

- **Risk-Return Tradeoff**

The link between the degree of risk taken and the possible returns anticipated from an investment is demonstrated by the risk-return tradeoff, a key concept in finance.

Important points consist of:

1- Greater risk, and higher potential profits: Investing in higher-risk securities can potentially yield higher profits, which would offset the additional risk that investors are taking on.

2- Diversification: By distributing risk and lessening the influence of any one asset's performance on the returns of the entire portfolio, investments made across a variety of asset classes, industries, and geographical areas can help manage risk.

3- Risk Tolerance: Selecting an asset allocation plan that suits your financial goals and degree of comfort with volatility requires an understanding of your risk tolerance and investment objectives.

- **Asset Allocation**

Distributing investments among several asset classes, including cash, bonds, stocks, and alternative investments, is known as asset allocation. This process aims to control risk and attain diversification.

Important tenets comprise

1- Risk management: During market downturns, distributing assets among several asset classes with differing degrees of risk and return potential helps reduce portfolio volatility and protect money.

2- Long-Term Goals: Match the distribution of assets to your time horizon, risk tolerance, and long-term financial objectives. For growth potential, younger investors with longer time horizons might allocate a larger percentage to stocks, whereas older investors might be more concerned with capital preservation through fixed-income investments.

3- Rebalancing: To preserve target asset allocation percentages and make adjustments for shifts in market circumstances or investment performance, evaluate and rebalance portfolio allocations regularly. Rebalancing makes sure that, over time, the portfolio stays in line with your investing goals and risk tolerance.

- **Understanding Market Cycles**

Making wise investment decisions and modifying portfolio allocations requires an understanding of market cycles and economic trends.

Important things to think about are:

1- Business cycle: Identify the expansion, peak, contraction, and trough phases of the business cycle and modify your asset allocation and investment plans accordingly.

2- Market valuations: Keep an eye on market valuations to determine whether companies are overpriced or undervalued based on historical averages. These valuation measurements include price-to-earnings ratios and others. Based on market forecasts and value levels, adjust the allocation of assets.

3- Economic Indicators: To assess the state of the economy and predict future changes in market circumstances, keep an eye on important economic indicators, including GDP growth, unemployment rates, inflation, and interest rates.

4- Diversification: To lower concentration risk and lessen the effect of particular market cycles or economic events on the performance of the entire portfolio, keep your portfolio well-diversified across asset classes and geographical areas.

Investors can maximize risk-adjusted returns and reach their long-term financial objectives by comprehending the risk-return tradeoff, putting efficient asset allocation methods into practice, and adjusting investments to market cycles.

Sub-Chapter 2: Behavioral Finance

- **Psychology and Investing**

Psychological factors have a big impact on how investors behave and make decisions.

Important details consist of:

1- Emotional Biases: Buying or selling assets based on short-term market swings rather than long-term fundamentals can result in irrational financial decisions. Examples of these emotions are fear, greed, and overconfidence.

2- Herd Mentality: Rather than using independent research or sound judgment, investors may fall victim to herd mentality and follow the herd while making investing decisions.

3- Loss Aversion: Investors typically feel more pain from losses than joy from winnings, which makes them risk-averse and more likely to hang onto losing investments rather than reallocating funds to more promising prospects and lowering losses.

- **Overcoming Cognitive Biases**

Adherence to rational investment principles, self-awareness, and discipline are necessary for mitigating cognitive biases.

Crucial tactics consist of:

1- Knowledge and awareness: Acquaint yourself with the typical cognitive biases and psychological pitfalls that may sway financial choices. Recognizing and combating these biases can be made easier with awareness of them.

2- Creating a Process: Come up with a methodical approach to investing that is grounded in in-depth investigation, impartial evaluation, and meticulous standards for making decisions. Respect your investing plan and refrain from acting on the spur of the moment in response to market noise or feelings.

3- Searching for Diverse Viewpoints and Independent Analysis To test your hypotheses and prevent succumbing to confirmation bias—the propensity to look for data that supports preexisting opinions or biases—seek out independent perspectives and independent analysis from reliable sources.

- **Long-Term Investing Mindset**

To succeed in investments and weather short-term market volatility, one must have a disciplined, long-term investing approach.

Important ideas consist of:

1- Concentrate on the fundamentals: Rather than relying solely on cyclical price swings, make investment selections based on underlying fundamentals, including firm earnings, cash flow, competitive positioning, and long-term growth prospects.

2- Patience and persistence: Acknowledge that these qualities are necessary for successful investing. Instead of attempting to anticipate the market or chase fads, concentrate on assembling a diverse portfolio of superior assets over the long term.

3- Staying the Course: Despite market volatility or economic uncertainty, stick to your investing plan and be diligent. Keep your long-term financial goals in mind and refrain from making rash decisions based on erratic market swings.

Investors can improve their capacity to reach their financial objectives and confidently negotiate the intricacies of the financial markets by comprehending the psychological aspects influencing investment decisions, putting these factors into practice, and adopting a disciplined, long-term investing mindset.

Sub-Chapter 3: Alternative Investment

• Real Estate Investing

The purpose of real estate investing is to generate income and/or capital appreciation through the purchase, ownership, management, and/or rental of properties.

Important advantages and difficulties consist of

1- Income Generation: A consistent stream of rental income from rental properties is something that can be especially alluring during a period of low-interest rates or a downturn in the economy.

2- Capital Appreciation: Historically, the value of real estate has increased over time, providing the possibility of long-term capital gains as property values rise.

3- Diversification: Since real estate investments don't correlate well with bonds and stocks, they're a useful instrument for lowering portfolio risk overall.

4- Leverage: When buying properties, real estate investors might use borrowed cash as leverage, which could increase returns but also raise risk and financial leverage.

5- Liquidity and Management: Compared to stocks and bonds, real estate investments are more illiquid, necessitating time and effort for the purchase, upkeep, and disposal of the asset. Property management can be difficult and include extra expenses and duties.

- ## Cryptocurrency and Blockchain

Blockchain technology and cryptocurrency have come to light as cutting-edge alternatives to traditional assets. They have the potential to yield large returns, but they also come with increased volatility and regulatory uncertainty.

Important things to think about are:

1- Decentralization: Peer-to-peer transactions, security, and transparency are provided by decentralized blockchain networks, which power cryptocurrencies like Ethereum and Bitcoin. These networks also eliminate the need for middlemen.

2- Volatility: The prices of cryptocurrencies fluctuate a lot, often due to variables including macroeconomic conditions, regulatory changes, market sentiment, and technological breakthroughs.

3- Diversification: By adding cryptocurrencies to a diverse investment portfolio, one may increase total portfolio diversification by gaining exposure to a new asset class that has no link to established financial markets.

4- Risk factors: Investing in cryptocurrencies carries special risks, such as those related to technology, cybersecurity, regulations, and liquidity. Taking into account their risk tolerance and financial goals, investors should do extensive research and proceed with caution when making cryptocurrency investments.

- **Precious metals and commodities**

Commodities and precious metals are examples of alternative assets that can be used to diversify portfolios and protect against inflation and currency depreciation.

Important details consist of:

1- Gold and silver: Throughout history, people have utilized precious metals like gold and silver as safe havens against inflation and unstable international markets. They could act as a buffer against unstable economies and inflation.

2- Commodities: Investing in commodities can expose one to inflationary pressures and worldwide economic trends. Examples of commodities include metals, oil, and natural gas. Because of their generally low correlation with conventional financial assets, commodities are a useful instrument for diversification.

3- Risk Factors: There are several risks associated with investing in commodities and precious metals, including supply-demand dynamics, price volatility, geopolitical unrest, and regulatory changes.

Investment strategy and portfolio allocation should be carefully considered by investors as they evaluate these risks. Investors can potentially increase long-term returns, diversify their portfolios, and reduce risk by looking at alternative investments, including real estate, cryptocurrencies, precious metals, and commodities.

To make the best investments, you must, however, match your risk tolerance and financial objectives with your investments, do extensive research, and comprehend the special traits and hazards associated with each asset type.

Sub-chapter 4: Income-generating investments

- **Dividend Stocks**

Stocks that pay dividends are those owned by businesses that provide shareholders with a portion of their profits in the form of dividends. Among the benefits of dividend stock investing are:

1- Regular Income: For retirees or investors who are focused on their income, dividend stocks are especially appealing since they offer a steady stream of income.

2- Prospect for expansion: Businesses that distribute dividends frequently have consistent cash flow and earnings, which suggests sound financial standing and room for expansion over the long run.

3- Dividend Growth: Over time, a lot of corporations raise their dividends, giving investors access to rising income streams and perhaps capital gains.

4- Portfolio Stability: Because dividend income can counteract share price drops, dividend-paying stocks can help keep a portfolio stable during market downturns.

- ## Bonds and Fixed-Income Investments

Debt instruments such as bonds and fixed-income investments guarantee investors a return of principal at maturity together with regular interest payments.

Important things to think about are:

1- Income Stability: Bonds are a good option for investors looking to preserve cash and receive a steady income because they pay interest at a known rate.

2- Diversification: By counteracting the volatility of stocks and other riskier assets, bonds can lower the overall risk of an investment portfolio when they are included.

3- Interest Rate Sensitivity: Bond prices and interest rates have an inverse relationship, which means that when interest rates rise, bond prices often fall and vice versa. When purchasing bonds, investors need to take interest rate risk into account.

4- Credit Risk: While bonds issued by lesser-ranked entities may involve a higher credit risk, bonds issued by governments or highly rated enterprises often have a lower credit risk.

- ## REITs and MLPs

Two alternative investment forms that provide prospects for income generation are master limited partnerships (MLPs) and real estate investment trusts (REITs).

Important elements consist of:

1- Real Estate Investment Trusts (REITs): REITs invest in real estate and pay out dividends to shareholders, which represent a sizable amount of their revenue. Without requiring actual property ownership, REITs give investors exposure to real estate assets.

2- Master Limited Partnerships (MLPs): MLPs are partnerships that are listed on public markets and that function in industries including infrastructure, real estate, and energy. The processing, storage, and transportation of commodities, such as natural resources, are the usual sources of revenue for MLPs.

3- Tax Considerations: Both REITs and MLPs have distinct tax advantages, such as pass-through taxation and tax-deferred distributions. Investors should, however, carefully consider the tax implications and seek advice from a tax adviser before investing.

4- Risk Factors: REITs and MLPs face unique risks such as interest rate risk, market volatility, regulatory changes, and industry-specific issues.Investors should do extensive study and due diligence before investing in these alternative asset classes.

Income-generating investments such as dividend stocks, bonds, REITs, and MLPs can help investors diversify their income sources, manage risk, and achieve their financial goals.

Sub-Chapter 5: Sustainable and Socially Responsible Investment

- **ESG Criteria**

Investors use environmental, social, and governance (ESG) standards to assess the sustainability and ethical impact of investments.

Important things to think about are:

1- Environmental Factors: Evaluating the effects of a business on the environment, including waste management, energy efficiency, carbon emissions, and the preservation of natural resources.

2- Social Factors: Assessing the social effect of a business, encompassing community involvement, human rights, diversity and inclusion, labor practices, and product safety.

3- Governance factors include looking at the executive pay scale, board makeup, transparency, and shareholder responsibility of a business.

4- Integration with the investing process: By incorporating environmental, social, and governance (ESG) standards into the investing process, investors can find businesses that exhibit ethical leadership and robust sustainability processes, which can lower risk and increase long-term returns.

- **Impact Investing**

Impact investing is putting money into businesses, groups, or initiatives that not only produce financial returns but also have a good social or environmental impact.

Important elements consist of:

1- Impact investing aims to match investments with investors' personal values and societal aspirations, while also achieving financial returns and positive social or environmental results.

2- Impact investors focus on industries where investments can solve urgent social or environmental issues, such as clean technology, affordable housing, sustainable agriculture, healthcare, and education.

3- Measurement and Reporting: Impact investors track and report on the social and environmental effects of their investments using metrics and frameworks like the Global Impact Investing Network (GIIN) standards and the United Nations Sustainable Development Goals (SDGs).

Balancing Returns and Ethics:

Balancing financial returns with ethical issues necessitates a thoughtful evaluation of investing objectives, risk tolerance, and impact goals.

- **Key strategies include**

1- Integrated Approach: Look for investment possibilities that meet both financial goals and ethical principles, taking into account ESG performance, impact measurements, and stakeholder participation.

2- Engagement and advocacy: Actively engage with businesses and investment managers to promote sustainable business practices, open governance, and positive social impact. Shareholder activism and proxy voting can influence business conduct and effect beneficial change.

3- Risk Management: Assess the financial and non-financial risks associated with impact investments, such as regulatory, reputational, and market hazards.

Diversify your investments across industries and asset classes to reduce risk and build resilience.

4- Long-Term Perspective: When pursuing impact investing methods, keep in mind that social and environmental effects may take time to manifest and that sustainable business practices can help to improve long-term financial performance.

By incorporating sustainable and socially responsible investing concepts into their investment strategies, investors can align their portfolios with their values, contribute to positive social and environmental change, and potentially earn competitive long-term financial returns.

Chapter 5: Understanding Debt and Credit

Subchapter 1: Understanding Debt

- **Types of Debt**

Debt falls into two categories: good debt and bad debt. Understanding the differences is critical for making sound financial decisions.

Good debt is debt that is utilized to fund investments or assets that have the potential to increase in value over time or create income. **<u>Examples include:</u>**
1- Student loans: Investing in education might result in increased earning potential and employment options.
2- Mortgage: Buying a home allows you to create equity while also providing stability and long-term financial security.
3- Business loans: Funding a business initiative might result in revenue and wealth over time.

Bad debt is debt used to finance items that do not increase in value and may impede financial success. **Examples are:**

Credit card debt: Carrying high-interest credit card debt for non-essential expenditures can cause financial hardship and hefty interest rates.

Payday loans: These short-term, high-interest loans are frequently employed for emergency necessities and can trap borrowers in a debt cycle.

- **Debt Repayment Strategies**

Individuals who use effective debt repayment plans can better manage their debt and achieve financial freedom.

Snowball Method: Begin by paying off the smallest debt first, then make minimum payments on the other obligations. Once the smallest debt is paid off, apply the amount paid to the next smallest loan, resulting in a snowball effect.

The Avalanche Method: Prioritize debts with the highest interest rates first to reduce interest payments over time. Make the minimum payment on all obligations while allocating more funds to the debt with the highest interest rate.

Debt Consolidation: Combine various loans into a single loan with a lower interest rate, making them easier to manage and perhaps lowering total interest expenses.

Increase Income and Reduce Expenses: Increase income by starting a side hustle or looking for ways to enhance wages. Create a budget, minimize wasteful spending, and renegotiate payments to save money.

- **Debt Consolidation and Refinancing:**

Debt consolidation and refinancing can help streamline debt repayment while potentially lowering interest expenses.

1- Debt Consolidation Loans: Combine several debts into a single loan with a lower interest rate, making repayment easier and perhaps lowering overall interest expenses.

2- Balance Transfer Credit Cards: Transfer high-interest credit card debt to a card with a reduced promotional interest rate, freeing up funds for principal repayment.

3- Home Equity Loans or Lines of Credit: Use your home equity to consolidate debt or finance large purchases. These options may have cheaper borrowing rates but require collateral.

4- Debt Management Programs: Collaborate with credit counseling services to develop a debt management strategy, which may include negotiating lower interest rates or payment arrangements with creditors.

Individuals can get control of their finances and work toward a debt-free future by recognizing the many types of debt, implementing efficient debt repayment techniques, and researching debt consolidation and refinancing possibilities.

Subchapter 2: Building and Maintaining Credit

- **Credit scores**

Credit scores are numerical representations of an individual's creditworthiness that lenders use to determine the risk of giving credit.

Key points include:

1- Credit ratings are important since they help determine eligibility for loans, credit cards, mortgages, and other financial goods. Higher credit scores often lead to cheaper interest rates and better lending terms.

2- Credit scores are calculated using characteristics such as payment history, credit utilization, duration of credit history, categories of credit, and new credit inquiries. Credit scores can be improved by making on-time payments and using credit responsibly.

3- Credit scores normally vary between 300 and 850, with higher scores indicating reduced credit risk. FICO scores are the most widely used credit scoring models, followed by VantageScore.

4- Credit scores have an impact on many elements of financial life, including loan approvals, interest rates, insurance premiums, rental applications, and employment chances.

• Credit Building Strategies

Building and maintaining a strong credit profile necessitates proactive management and responsible credit behavior.

Strategies include:

1- Pay Bills on Time: To develop a positive payment history avoid late payment penalties and poor credit reports, and pay bills on time consistently.

2- Monitor credit reports: Check your credit reports from the major credit agencies (Equifax, Experian, and TransUnion) regularly for errors, discrepancies, and fraudulent activity. To keep your credit information correct, instantly dispute any errors.

3- Manage Credit Utilization: Keep credit card balances low in comparison to credit limits to maintain a low credit utilization ratio, ideally below 30% of available credit. High credit utilization can harm credit ratings.

4- Diversify credit types: To demonstrate responsible credit management and boost credit scores, keep a mix of credit types, including revolving credit (credit cards) and installment loans (mortgages and auto loans).

5- Limit the quantity of new credit applications and inquiries to avoid any negative impact on credit ratings. Multiple queries in a short period can indicate financial distress to lenders.

- ## Credit Monitoring Tools

Credit monitoring tools allow people to follow their credit scores, receive alerts about changes to their credit reports, and detect potential symptoms of identity theft or fraud.

Key tools include:

1- Enroll in credit monitoring services provided by credit bureaus, financial institutions, and third-party suppliers. These services give regular credit score updates, credit report adjustments, and alerts to suspect activity.

2- Credit Score Apps: Download mobile apps that provide free access to credit scores and credit monitoring tools, allowing users to watch their credit health while on the go and receive real-time notifications about critical credit occurrences.

3- credit monitoring: Consider signing up for identity theft protection services, which provide credit monitoring, identity theft insurance, and resolution support in the event of identity theft or fraud.

4- Annual Credit Reports: AnnualCreditReport.com provides free annual credit reports for reviewing credit history, checking for inaccuracies, and monitoring changes to credit accounts.

Individuals who understand the importance of credit scores, implement credit-building strategies, and use credit monitoring tools can take proactive steps to build and maintain a healthy credit profile, gain access to favorable financial opportunities, and achieve their long-term financial goals.

Sub-Chapter 3: Smart borrowing

- **Loan review**

1- Before applying for a loan, individuals should thoroughly analyze their financial condition and consider issues such as:

2- Determining the loan's purpose and whether it is consistent with financial goals and priorities. Consider whether the loan is necessary and if there are other financial choices available.

3- Review the loan's terms and conditions, such as interest rates, fees, payback terms, and any potential fines or charges. Compare offers from various lenders to discover the best rates.

4- Repayability: Determine your ability to repay the loan based on your existing income, expenses, and financial responsibilities. Calculate your debt-to-income ratio to guarantee that your monthly loan payments are affordable.

5- Credit Score and Credit History: Recognize the potential effects of your credit score and credit history on interest rates and loan eligibility. If required, take action to increase creditworthiness before the loan application.

- ## Interest Rate Negotiation

Negotiating interest rates can help consumers get better loan conditions and save money throughout the loan.

Here are some tips for negotiating interest rates:

1- Shop around: Compare interest rates and loan offers from several lenders to take advantage of competing offers and negotiate better terms.

2- Highlight Strong Credit: To negotiate lower borrowing rates, emphasize your strong credit history and creditworthiness. Provide evidence of competent financial management and early debt payback.

3- Negotiate Charges: In addition to interest rates, negotiate fees, origination charges, and other loan-related expenditures to lower overall borrowing costs.

4- Consider Prepayment Alternatives: Find out about prepayment alternatives and penalties for early repayment. Choose loans that offer flexible repayment options and a penalty-free early payoff.

• Leveraging Credit for Investments

While borrowing money to invest might increase earnings, it also carries dangers and must be carefully considered. Responsible ways to use credit for wealth-building include:

1- Investment Diversification: To reduce risk and increase returns, allocate borrowed funds to diversified investment portfolios that include a range of asset classes, sectors, and risk profiles.

2- Risk management entails weighing investment risk and prospective returns before borrowing funds to invest. Avoid speculative investments and high-risk techniques that could result in losses or financial instability.

3- Cash Flow Analysis: Perform a detailed cash flow analysis to guarantee that investment returns surpass borrowing expenses and loan payback obligations. When analyzing investment prospects, consider probable market swings and interest rate adjustments.

4- Monitoring and Adjustment: Regularly assess investment performance and alter strategies as needed to reduce risks and capitalize on market opportunities. Maintain discipline and prevent overleveraging or taking unnecessary risks with borrowed funds.

Individuals can make informed borrowing decisions to support their long-term financial goals and objectives by carefully reviewing loans, negotiating advantageous conditions, and properly using credit for wealth-building possibilities.

Subchapter 4: Debt-Free Strategies

- **Debt Snowball vs. Debt Avalanche**

The debt snowball and the debt avalanche are two prominent debt repayment tactics.

Key differences include:

1- Debt Snowball: The debt snowball strategy entails repaying bills in order of lowest to greatest balance, regardless of interest rates. The goal is to get rapid wins and gain momentum by tackling minor debts first.

2- Debt Avalanche: The debt avalanche technique prioritizes paying off the debts with the highest interest rates first while making minimal payments on the other bills. This technique reduces overall interest expenses and may lead to faster debt payback.

• The Psychology of Debt Freedom

Debt relief has far-reaching emotional and psychological consequences in addition to financial rewards.

The psychology of debt liberation encompasses

1- Reduced Stress and worry: Paying off debt can relieve financial stress and worry, resulting in better mental health and well-being.

2- Increased Confidence and Empowerment: Being debt-free allows people to take charge of their finances and make informed decisions. It increases confidence and self-esteem, resulting in increased financial resilience.

3- Debt independence allows you to pursue your goals, desires, and opportunities without being burdened by debt responsibilities. It creates opportunities for travel, career changes, entrepreneurship, and personal development.

• Creating a Debt-Free Plan

Creating a personalized debt-free plan requires the following steps:

1- Assessing Debt: Create a detailed list of all debts, including balances, interest rates, minimum payments, and payback conditions.

2- Setting Goals: Establish clear, quantifiable debt payback goals, such as paying off high-interest bills, being debt-free by a specified date, or meeting a target debt-to-income ratio.

3- Choosing a Strategy: Choose a debt repayment strategy based on your personal preferences, financial goals, and available resources. Consider interest rates, debt levels, and psychological reasons.

4- Creating a Budget: Create a realistic budget that allocates monies for debt repayment while also covering necessary expenses and saving goals. Track spending, identify cost-cutting opportunities, and prioritize debt payments.

5- Staying Motivated: To stay motivated and focused on long-term goals, celebrate milestones, visualize progress, and seek help from friends, family, or support groups.

Individuals can make proactive efforts toward debt elimination, financial independence, and a more secure future by evaluating debt repayment alternatives, understanding the psychology of debt freedom, and developing a tailored debt-free strategy.

Sub-chapter 5: Credit and Identity Theft Prevention

- ### Credit Freeze and Monitoring

Credit freezes and monitoring are proactive methods that protect against identity theft and illegal access to credit data.

The key points include:

1- Credit Freeze: Place a credit freeze (also known as a security freeze) on credit reports to limit access to credit data. A credit freeze stops lenders from accessing credit reports, making it difficult for identity thieves to register new accounts under your name.

2- Credit monitoring: Enroll in credit monitoring services to receive notifications about changes to your credit report, such as new accounts, credit inquiries, or suspicious activity. Credit monitoring allows you to spot potential symptoms of identity theft early and take timely action.

- ### Identity Theft Resolution

If identity theft happens, use these procedures to minimize harm and restore creditworthiness

1- Report identity theft: Contact the Federal Trade Commission (FTC) and file an identity theft report with local law enforcement. Maintain copies of all correspondence and documentation for future reference.

2- Notify credit bureaus: Contact the major credit bureaus (Equifax, Experian, and TransUnion) to post fraud warnings on credit reports and obtain copies to review for unauthorized activity.

3- Dispute fraudulent charges: Contact your creditors and financial institutions to dispute any bogus charges or accounts. Provide supporting paperwork, such as identity theft reports and affidavits, to prove your claim.

4- Monitor Credit: Constantly check credit reports and accounts for any signs of fraudulent activity. Consider enrolling in identity theft protection services to ensure continual monitoring and help.

- ## Legal Protections: Explore the Legal Tools

Available for Credit Protection Consumers have legal protections and rights under numerous laws and regulations to protect themselves against identity theft and fraudulent activities.

<u>**Important legal protections include**</u>

1- The Fair Credit Reporting Act (FCRA) governs the collection, transmission, and use of consumer credit information and includes options for contesting inaccurate or fraudulent information on credit reports.

2- The Fair and Accurate Credit Transactions Act (FACTA) gives consumers the right to get free annual credit reports, place fraud alerts, and request credit freezes to avoid identity theft.

3- Identity Theft and Assumption Deterrence Act: This federal law makes it a crime to intentionally transfer or use another person's identity for illegal purposes, such as identity theft or fraud.

Chapter 6: Tax Efficiency and Wealth Preservation

Sub-Chapter 1: Understanding Tax Systems

- ### Tax Basics

Understanding the fundamentals of income taxation is critical for successful tax planning and wealth preservation.

The key points include

income tax, capital gains tax, inheritance tax, and gift tax, which are some of the various forms of taxes that might be discussed.

1- Tax Filing Status: Explain the various tax filing statuses, including single, married filing jointly, married filing separately, and head of household, and how they affect tax liabilities.

2- Taxable Income: Define taxable income and explore taxable sources of income such as earnings, salaries, interest, dividends, capital gains, and rentals.

3- Tax Rates and Brackets: Explain how tax rates and brackets operate, including progressive tax systems in which tax rates rise with income.

- **Tax Deductions and Credits**

Tax deductions and credits allow taxpayers to lower their taxable income and total tax burden.

The key concepts include:

1- Tax Deductions: Explain how tax deductions reduce taxable income and explore common ones, including mortgage interest, property taxes, charitable contributions, and qualified business costs.

2- Tax Credits: Define tax credits, which are dollar-for-dollar reductions in tax burden, and highlight notable credits such as the Earned Income Tax Credit (EITC), Child Tax Credit, and Education Credit.

3- Above-the-line deductions: Consider above-the-line deductions, which are removed from gross income to determine adjusted gross income (AGI), such as retirement contributions, health savings account (HSA) payments, and self-employment taxes.

- **Tax-Advantaged Accounts**

Tax-advantaged investment accounts provide chances to increase wealth while reducing tax liabilities.

Key account types are:

1- Retirement Accounts: Discuss tax-deferred retirement accounts like traditional IRAs, 401(k) plans, and other employer-sponsored retirement plans that allow contributions to grow tax-free until withdrawn.

2- Roth Accounts: Explain Roth IRAs and Roth 401(k)s, which provide tax-free growth and withdrawals for eligible distributions, making them ideal for long-term retirement savings.

3- Introduce Health Savings Accounts (HSAs), which provide three tax benefits: donations are tax-deductible, profits grow tax-free, and eligible withdrawals for medical costs are tax-free.

4- Education Savings Accounts: Emphasize tax-favored accounts that provide tax-free growth and withdrawals for eligible educational expenses, such as Coverdell Education Savings Accounts (ESAs) and 529 plans.

People can maximize their tax efficiency and protect wealth for future financial objectives by knowing the fundamentals of taxation, taking advantage of credits and deductions, and making good use of tax-advantaged accounts.

Sub-Chapter 2: Tax Planning Strategies

- ## Year-round Tax Planning

Year-round consideration of financial choices and their tax ramifications is necessary for effective tax planning.

Important tactics consist of:

1- Keeping an Eye on Tax Law Changes: Revisions to tax laws and regulations may have an impact on contribution caps, credits, deductions, and tax planning techniques.

2- Maximize retirement contributions: To lower taxable income and increase retirement savings, take advantage of tax-advantaged retirement accounts and contribute the maximum amount permitted each year.

3- Harvest Tax Losses and Gains: To reduce tax obligations on investment returns, use tax-loss harvesting techniques to offset capital gains with capital losses.

4- Control Timing of Income and Spending: To maximize tax results, schedule the time of income recognition and deductible spending. To reduce taxable income in high-income years, think about delaying income or increasing expenses.

- **Professional Assistance**

Professional tax guidance can give invaluable insights and skills in optimizing tax planning methods and ensuring tax compliance.

Important factors to consider are:

1- Consult skilled tax consultants, such as certified public accountants (CPAs), enrolled agents (EAs), or tax attorneys, for specialized tax advice targeted to your specific financial circumstances and goals.

2- Tax Planning Services: Use tax planning services provided by financial advisors, asset managers, or tax professionals to create comprehensive tax plans that are linked to long-term financial goals.

3- Tax Preparation: Hire expert tax preparers to precisely prepare and file tax returns, ensuring compliance with complicated tax laws and regulations and maximizing possible tax.

- **Tax-Efficient Withdrawal Strategies**

Tax-efficient withdrawal techniques can help retirees maximize their income while reducing their tax responsibilities.

The key strategies are as follows:

1-:Roth Conversion: Consider progressively converting traditional retirement account balances to Roth accounts, especially during years with reduced income or tax rates. Roth conversions can generate tax-free income during retirement and reduce future required minimum distributions (RMDs).

2- Asset Allocation: To maximize tax efficiency, divide assets strategically among taxable, tax-deferred, and tax-free accounts. Put tax-efficient investments like equities and index funds in taxable accounts and tax-inefficient investments like bonds and REITs in tax-advantaged retirement accounts.

3- Systematic Withdrawals: Use systematic withdrawal procedures to balance income demands and tax considerations. Withdraw from taxable accounts first, then tax-deferred accounts, and finally tax-free accounts, keeping in mind RMD requirements and tax brackets.

4- Social Security Optimization: Combine Social Security claiming tactics with retirement account withdrawals to reduce long-term taxation. Delaying Social Security benefits might raise monthly income and protect against longevity risk.

Individuals can improve their tax outcomes, conserve wealth, and achieve their long-term financial goals by using proactive tax planning methods, seeking expert tax counsel when necessary, and investigating tax-efficient withdrawal strategies after retirement.

Subchapter 3: Estate Planning

- **Importance of Estate Planning**

Estate planning is important for lots of reasons, including

1- Asset Protection: Estate planning protects assets from unwanted taxes, creditors, and probable legal issues, preserving money for intended beneficiaries.

2- Control and Decision-Making: Estate planning allows individuals to retain control of their assets and make key decisions about their distribution, guardianship of minor children, and healthcare preferences in the event of incapacity.

3- Avoiding Probate: By using mechanisms such as trusts and beneficiary designations, proper estate planning can help avoid the time-consuming, expensive, and public probate procedure.

4- Family Harmony: Estate planning enables individuals to properly explain their preferences, reducing conflicts and misunderstandings among family members and ensuring that their legacy is kept as planned.

- **Wills and Trusts**

Wills and trusts are essential estate planning vehicles that serve different purposes:

Wills: Wills are legal documents that detail how a person's assets and properties should be transferred after their death. It also assigns guardians for minor children and an executor to oversee the estate. Will go through the probate procedure, which varies in complexity and length based on state legislation.

Trusts: A trust is a legal body that holds and manages assets for the benefit of its beneficiaries. Trusts, unlike wills, can avoid probate, giving you more privacy, efficiency, and flexibility when distributing your assets. Trusts can also provide other benefits, such as asset protection, incapacity planning, and tax savings.

- **Legacy Planning**

Legacy planning is more than just distributing money; it also includes passing on beliefs, traditions, and philanthropic aims to future generations. Important parts of legacy planning include:

1- Family Values and Stories: Recording family histories, values, and customs ensures that they are preserved and passed down to future generations, reinforcing family relationships and identity.

2- Philanthropy: By including charity giving into estate plans, individuals can leave a long-term effect on causes and organizations that share their values and passions, building a giving culture within the family.

3- Education and Empowerment: Providing resources for education, entrepreneurship, or personal development enables future generations to grow and succeed, building on the family's tradition of achievement and philanthropy.

Sub-Chapter 4: Wealth Transfer Strategies

- **Gifting Strategies**

Gifting is a tax-efficient method of transferring wealth during one's lifetime while minimizing possible estate tax penalties.

The key gifting strategies include:

1- Annual Gift Exclusion: Use the annual gift tax exclusion to gift up to a specified amount (as established by the IRS) per recipient each year without paying gift tax or claiming the lifetime estate tax exemption.

2- Take advantage of the lifetime gift tax exemption, which allows individuals to give away a set amount (as determined by the IRS) over their lifetime without incurring gift tax.

3- Direct Payments: Make payments on behalf of recipients for medical, tuition, or educational expenditures that are exempt from gift tax and do not count toward the annual or lifetime gift tax exclusions.

- ## Charitable Giving

Charitable donations not only help deserving causes, but they also provide financial and tax benefits.
Important concerns for charity giving include:
1- Donor-advised monies (DAFs): Create a DAF to centralize charitable giving, receive immediate tax deductions for contributions, and distribute monies to charity gradually.
2- Qualified Charitable Distributions (QCDs) allow retirees to make tax-efficient charitable contributions by directing IRA distributions to qualified charities after reaching the age of 70.
3- Endowment Funds and Planned Giving: Establish endowment funds or employ planned giving methods like charitable remainder trusts (CRTs) or charitable lead trusts (CLTs) to assist charitable causes while maximizing tax benefits and creating a lasting legacy.

- ## Succession Planning for Businesses

To sustain continuity and preserve riches for future generations, family-owned businesses must plan their succession carefully.
Key components of succession planning are:

1- Identifying Successors: Identify possible successors within the family or business and provide training, mentoring, and development opportunities to prepare them for leadership positions.

2- Developing a Succession Plan: Create a comprehensive succession plan that details the transfer of ownership and management duties, accounts for tax implications, and minimizes disruptions to business operations.

3- Estate Equalization: To minimize disagreements and promote family unity, use techniques to equalize inheritances among heirs, especially when some are involved in the family company and others are not.

Sub-chapter 5: Protecting Wealth During Economic Downturns

- ## Diversification for Stability

Diversification is a critical approach for decreasing investment risk and protecting capital during market downturns.

<u>**The key diversification strategies are:**</u>

1- Asset Allocation: To spread risk and limit exposure to market volatility, distribute assets among a variety of asset classes such as stocks, bonds, real estate, and alternative investments.

2- Geographic Diversification: Invest in a globally diversified portfolio to reduce country-specific risks and capitalize on opportunities in various locations and markets.

3- Sector Diversification: Spread assets across multiple sectors and industries to reduce concentration risk and mitigate the impact of sector-specific downturns on portfolio performance.

4- Consider alternative assets such as precious metals, commodities, and hedge funds, which may have a low correlation with traditional asset classes and provide diversification benefits during volatile market periods.

- **Insurance as a precaution**

Insurance is critical for protecting wealth and managing the financial risks associated with unforeseen catastrophes.

The key insurance strategies are:

1- Purchasing life insurance coverage to provide financial security for loved ones in the event of early death, ensuring that beneficiaries have enough money to maintain their standard of living and pay for expenditures.

2- Disability Insurance: Purchase disability insurance to replace lost income and pay living expenses in the event of a disabling disease or injury, protecting yourself from the financial effects of a temporary or permanent disability.

3- Long-Term Care Insurance: Consider long-term care insurance to cover the costs of medical and personal care services for chronic illnesses or disabilities that may develop in later life, thereby safeguarding retirement assets from depletion due to healthcare expenses.

- **Emergency Funds for Economic Resilience**

Maintaining an adequate emergency fund is critical for financial resilience and stability, particularly during economic downturns.

Important concerns for emergency finances are:

1- Fund Size: Set aside three to six months' worth of living expenses in an easily accessible emergency fund to cover unforeseen expenses, job losses, or income disruptions during an economic downturn.

2- Keep emergency assets in liquid and low-risk investments like high-yield savings accounts, money market funds, or short-term Treasury securities to assure quick access to cash when needed.

3- Regular Review and Replenishment: Check emergency fund balances regularly and replenish money as needed to account for changes in costs, income, or financial goals, ensuring that emergency reserves are adequate to meet changing demands.

Individuals can strengthen their financial situation, weather economic downturns with confidence, and retain wealth in the long run by diversifying their investments, using insurance for protection, and keeping appropriate emergency savings.

Chapter 7: Behavioral Finance Mastery

Subchapter 1: Emotional Intelligence in Finance

- **Emotional Resilience**

Emotional resilience is required for making wise financial decisions and navigating market fluctuations.

Key features include

1- Self-Awareness: Recognize and understand your emotions, triggers, and biases that may influence financial decisions, helping you to make more intentional choices.

2- Self-Regulation: Learn to manage and control emotions like fear, greed, and impulsivity to avoid making rash or unreasonable financial decisions.

3- Empathy: Understanding the emotions and viewpoints of others, such as family members, financial advisors, or market participants, can help you communicate and collaborate more effectively on financial problems.

4- Adaptability: Be flexible and adaptive in reaction to changing market conditions, unforeseen events, and financial setbacks, while remaining positive and resilient in the face of adversity.

- ## Managing Fear and Greed

Fear and greed are two frequent emotions that might cause investors to make irrational judgments amid market volatility.

Techniques for coping with these emotions include:

1- Rational Analysis: Make financial decisions based on rational analysis, study, and data rather than emotional reactions to short-term market trends or headlines.

2- Long-Term Perspective: Instead of reacting rashly to short-term market volatility, take a long-term investment approach and focus on your financial goals, objectives, and risk tolerance.

3- Dollar-Cost Averaging: Use a dollar-cost averaging method to invest consistently over time, independent of market volatility, and reduce the impact of emotional decision-making on investment results.

4- Seeking Support: During times of market volatility, surround yourself with a supportive network of friends, family, and financial professionals who can offer advice, perspective, and reassurance.

- **Mindfulness techniques**

Mindfulness techniques can help people develop a calm, focused, and non-reactive approach to financial decision-making.

Techniques include:

1- Breath Awareness: Practice mindful breathing techniques to help you stay in the present moment, reduce stress, and make better financial decisions.

2- Mindful Observation: Observe your thoughts, feelings, and experiences without judgment or attachment, resulting in increased self-awareness and detachment from impulsive or unreasonable financial impulses.

3- Gratitude Practice: Develop a positive mindset by being grateful for your financial resources, accomplishments, and opportunities. This will help you reduce thoughts of scarcity, fear, or being inadequate.

4- Visualization: Use guided visualization exercises to make your financial goals, objectives, and aspirations more concrete, attainable, and motivating.

Individuals can adopt a calm, focused, and disciplined attitude to financial decision-making by establishing emotional resilience, regulating fear and greed, and practicing mindfulness practices, which will result in more positive outcomes and improved financial well-being.

Sub-chapter 2: Setting and Achieving Financial Goals

- **SMART objectives**

Setting SMART goals is critical for developing clear, actionable, and inspiring targets that reflect your financial priorities and aspirations.

Key components of SMART goals are:
Specific: To create clarity and concentration, outline your financial goals in detail, including the desired outcome, quantity, and timescale.
Measurable: Create measurable criteria for tracking progress and evaluating achievements, such as monetary amounts, percentages, or milestones met.
Achievable: Set goals that are achievable given your existing financial status, resources, abilities, and time frame, rather than overly ambitious or impossible aims.
Relevant: Make sure your goals are relevant and significant to your financial values, priorities, and long-term ambitions, and that they are consistent with your entire financial strategy and life goals.

Time-bound: Establish clear deadlines or time frames for attaining your objectives, instilling a sense of urgency and accountability to take action and progress continuously.

- ## Goal Visualization

Visualization techniques can improve goal-setting success by including the subconscious mind and reinforcing desired results.

The steps for goal visualization are:

1- Create a mental image: Imagine yourself attaining your financial goals and feeling the emotions, sensations, and pleasures that come with it.

2- Engage Your Senses: Immerse yourself in the visualization process by envisioning how it will look, hear, feel, smell, and taste when you reach your financial goals.

3- Repetition and Affirmation: Use positive affirmations and visualizations frequently to reinforce your belief in your capacity to achieve your goals and overcome any doubts or hurdles that arise.

4- Visualization Techniques: Experiment with various visualization techniques, such as vision boards, guided imagery, and mental rehearsals, to identify the ones that work best for you and increase motivation and attention.

- **Goal tracking and modifications:**

Monitoring progress and making adjustments is critical for staying on track with your financial objectives and responding to new circumstances. Tools for goal tracking and changes include the following:

1- Financial Tracking Tools: Use budgeting applications, spreadsheets, or financial management software to track your income, expenses, savings, investments, and progress toward your goals.

Conduct regular evaluations of your financial goals and objectives, analyzing your progress, recognizing any roadblocks or issues, and adjusting your tactics or deadlines as needed.

2- Course Corrections: Be willing to make course corrections along the road, such as changing your spending habits, updating your savings goals, or reallocating investments, to stay on track with your changing financial circumstances and priorities.

3- Milestones and achievements should be celebrated along the way to reaffirm progress, sustain motivation, and recognize the effort and attention put into pursuing your financial goals.

Setting SMART objectives, envisioning desired results, and actively tracking progress while making adjustments as appropriate can help people boost their chances of success, stay motivated, and attain greater financial empowerment and fulfillment.

Subchapter 3: Behavioral Biases and Investment Pitfalls

- **Common Biases**

1- Confirmation bias: the tendency to seek out information that confirms previously held thoughts or attitudes, resulting in selective exposure and probable data misinterpretation.
2- Loss Aversion: The preference for avoiding losses over earning equal profits, which leads to risk aversion and the probable loss of advantageous investment possibilities.
3- Overconfidence bias: the propensity to overestimate one's abilities or knowledge, resulting in excessive risk-taking and poor financial decisions.
4- Anchoring bias: Anchoring bias is the tendency to make judgments based too heavily on initial knowledge or reference points, resulting in inefficient adjustments to changing market conditions.

- **Avoiding Investment Pitfalls**

1- Awareness: Recognize and acknowledge the presence of cognitive biases in financial decision-making, promoting increased self-awareness and mindfulness in investment choices.

2- Diversification: Use a diverse investment portfolio to lessen the influence of individual investment biases and lower total risk exposure.

3- Consultation: Seek feedback from trusted financial experts or peers to gain new views and challenge decision-making biases.

4- Decision Templates: Create decision-making frameworks or checklists to methodically examine investment prospects and reduce the impact of cognitive bias.

• Learning from Mistakes:

1- Reflection: Review past investment decisions on a regular basis, identifying successes, failures, and opportunities for improvement to help guide future investment strategies.

2- Adaptation: Adopt a growth attitude, viewing mistakes as opportunities for learning and growth rather than failures, and change your investment strategies accordingly.

3- Continuous Improvement: Make a commitment to continued education and self-improvement in financial literacy and investment knowledge, as well as remaining current on market trends and changing best practices.

Subchapter 4: Decision-Making Frameworks

- **Cost-Benefit Analysis**

1- Costs and advantages: Determine and quantify the prospective costs and advantages of each financial choice, including monetary, time, and opportunity costs.
2- Weighing Trade-offs: Weigh the costs and advantages, taking into account risk, return on investment, and alignment with long-term financial goals.
3- Decision Criteria: Determine acceptable expenses and desired benefits to guide the selection of the best solutions.

- **Pros and drawbacks Methodology**

1- List Pros and Cons: Taking into account both quantitative and qualitative factors, compile a thorough list of the potential benefits and drawbacks connected to each choice that is now available.
2- Weighting Factors: To enable a more nuanced assessment, give each pro and con a weight or priority based on their respective importance and relevance to the decision at hand.
3- Decision Matrix: To aid in decision-making, compile advantages and disadvantages and rank and

compare possibilities objectively. You can also use a scoring system for this purpose.

- **Seeking professional assistance**

Expert Guidance: To obtain insightful information, specialized knowledge, and recommendations that are specific to your financial circumstances and objectives, speak with licensed financial counselors or experts.

Gain an objective, unbiased viewpoint on investment possibilities and hazards by consulting a third party. This will help you overcome prejudices and steer clear of frequent decision-making traps.

Sub-chapter 5: Wealth Mindset Maintenance

- **Regular Financial Check-ins:**

1- Scheduled Reviews: Set aside time regularly, such as monthly or quarterly, to examine your financial objectives, investment portfolio, and overall financial health.

2- Performance Evaluation: review progress toward financial goals, review investment performance, and determine any necessary adjustments or reallocations to remain on track.

3- Budgeting and Spending Analysis: Examine income and expenses, find areas for potential savings or optimization, and alter budgeting procedures as needed to meet financial goals.

- **Adapting to Change**

1- Market Dynamics: Stay current on changes in market circumstances, economic trends, and regulatory developments that may affect investment plans or financial goals.
2- Life Events: Be prepared to adjust your financial plans and methods in reaction to significant life events such as marriage, parenthood, work changes, or unanticipated emergencies.
3- Risk Management: Constantly review and minimize threats to your financial well-being, such as investment risks, insurance coverage, and estate planning considerations, altering tactics as necessary to preserve resilience.

- **Appreciating achievements**

1- Recognition: Celebrate and acknowledge important turning points in your financial journey, such as accomplishing savings goals, debt repayment milestones, or investment milestones.
2- Positive Reinforcement: Highlight accomplishments to encourage sustained

advancement toward long-term objectives and to promote sound financial practices.

3- Gratitude: Develop an attitude of thankfulness for opportunities, resources, and financial advancement. This can help you feel good about yourself and reinforce your feelings of prosperity and success.

Chapter 8: Legacy-Building and Impactful Wealth

Sub-Chapter 1: Personal Legacy

- ### Legacy Beyond Wealth

1- Values and Principles: A person's legacy is the set of values, principles, beliefs, and life lessons that they impart to future generations to help shape who they are and how they behave.

2- Effect on Relationships: A person's legacy goes beyond their material possessions to encompass their family dynamics, their relationships, and their memories with their loved ones.

3- Contributions to Society: People can leave a lasting legacy through their charitable giving, voluntary labor, mentoring, and support of issues close to their hearts.

- ### Impact on Community

1- Community Engagement: By tackling social concerns and promoting empowerment and collaboration, active participation in local organizations, community initiatives, and philanthropic causes can have a positive effect on the community.

2- Leadership and Service: Volunteering, serving the community, and taking on leadership roles all support social cohesiveness, individual and family well-being, and community growth.

3- Legacy Projects: You can leave a lasting legacy that benefits both the present and future generations by taking on legacy projects like environmental protection, educational programs, or community development activities.

- ## Balancing Family and Legacy Objectives

1- Open Communication: Encourage open and honest communication among family members to discuss individual and collective legacy objectives, beliefs, and priorities, guaranteeing alignment and support.

2- Collaborative Decision-Making: Involve family members in the design and implementation of legacy projects to foster shared ownership and participation in activities that represent the family's values and goals.

3- Appreciate individual choices: recognize and appreciate family members' different interests, passions, and accomplishments, allowing them to follow their legacy route while maintaining family unity and harmony.

Sub-chapter 2: Philanthropic and Social Impact

• Strategic Philanthropy

1- Mission and Vision: Create clear mission and vision statements for philanthropic activities that outline the beliefs, aims, and expected outcomes of charity-giving projects.

2- Strategic Focus Areas: Determine strategic focus areas or causes that are consistent with your personal values, interests, and areas of competence, enabling more targeted and impactful charitable contributions.

3- Collaborative Partnerships: Form strategic alliances with nonprofits, community leaders, and stakeholders to maximize social impact by leveraging resources, knowledge, and networks.

• Creating Social Change

1- Systems Change: Address the underlying causes of social crises and inequities through systemic change initiatives, policy lobbying, and community mobilization efforts targeted at achieving long-term solutions.

2- Empowerment and Capacity Building: Invest in programs and projects that empower marginalized groups, increase capacity, and encourage self-sufficiency, building resilience and long-term positive change.

3- Social Innovation: Encourage innovative approaches to addressing social concerns, such as social entrepreneurship, technology-driven solutions, and cross-sector collaborations that result in good social change and transformation.

- ## Measuring charitable Impact

1- Outcome Measurement: Establish clear outcome metrics and indicators to evaluate the performance and impact of charitable activities, including quantitative and qualitative success measures.

2- Data Collection and Analysis: Gather and evaluate information on key performance indicators, program outcomes, and beneficiary input to monitor progress, identify areas for improvement, and guide strategic decision-making.

3- Learning and Adaptation: Foster a culture of learning and continuous improvement in philanthropy by sharing insights, best practices, and lessons learned to increase the effectiveness and efficiency of charitable giving over time.

Individuals can leave a lasting legacy that reflects their values, passions, and dedication to good global change by defining personal legacies beyond wealth, participating in strategic philanthropy and social impact activities, and monitoring the efficacy of charitable giving efforts.

Sub-Chapter 3: Sustainable and Ethical Investment

• Aligning Investments with Values

1- Personal Values: Help investors establish their essential values and beliefs, such as environmental sustainability, social justice, or corporate governance, and then align their investing selections appropriately.

2- Screening Criteria: Use screening criteria, such as environmental, social, and governance (ESG) variables, to evaluate the ethical and sustainability performance of businesses and investments, ensuring that they correspond with personal beliefs.

3- Ethical Investment Vehicles: Consider investing in ethical funds, socially responsible mutual funds, or impact investment possibilities that emphasize companies with beneficial environmental and social consequences, as well as projects that align with your values.

• Supporting Sustainable Practices

1- Environmental Responsibility: Invest in companies that promote environmental sustainability, renewable energy, conservation initiatives, and eco-friendly activities, thus promoting positive environmental outcomes and decreasing climate change concerns.

2- Social Responsibility: Encourage organizations that support social justice, diversity and inclusion, fair labor practices, community participation, and charity, thus creating social well-being and equity.

3- Corporate Governance: Assess organizations based on their governance processes, transparency, accountability, and ethical leadership, and invest in those with strong governance frameworks that promote shareholder interests and stakeholder participation.

- **Balancing rewards and values**

1- Long-Term Perspective: Recognize that sustainable and ethical investing can produce competitive long-term financial returns while also reflecting personal beliefs and social impact goals.

2- Risk-Return Profile: Evaluate the risk-return profile of ethical investments, taking into account aspects such as financial performance, market trends, legislative changes, and reputational risks connected with ethical failings or controversy.

3- Diversification: To manage risk, diversify investment portfolios across asset classes, industries, and locations, capturing the potential for both financial returns and ethical considerations that are consistent with personal values.

Sub-chapter 4: Passing on Financial Wisdom

• Financial Education for Heirs

1- Early Start: Introduce children to basic financial concepts such as budgeting, saving, investing, and responsible spending through age-appropriate activities and talks.

2- Hands-On Experience: Give heirs realistic experiences and opportunities to manage money, make financial decisions, and learn from real-world circumstances, allowing them to build financial literacy and confidence in handling their finances.

3- Mentorship: Serve as a mentor or guide for heirs, providing financial support, advice, and guidance while sharing personal experiences, lessons learned, and best practices for wealth creation and financial independence.

• Family Financial Meetings

1- Open Dialogue: Encourage honest and transparent communication within the family by scheduling frequent financial meetings to go over objectives, concerns, opportunities, and hurdles in estate planning, wealth management, and financial decision-making.

2- Empowerment and Education: To encourage responsibility and empowerment, use family gatherings as a chance to go over investment strategies, ask for opinions on family financial goals, and educate heirs about financial problems. You can also involve them in decision-making processes.

3- Conflict Resolution: To resolve potential disputes or arguments involving money, family members should work together to find mutually beneficial solutions by voicing their concerns and offering a constructive and collaborative approach.

- **Creating a Financial Legacy Plan**

1- Legacy Vision: Summarize the main goals, values, and impact of the financial legacy plan. It also outlines the values and guiding principles that will help preserve and transmit money between generations.

2- Wealth Transfer Strategies: Create plans to transfer assets to heirs in a way that minimizes estate taxes and is both equitable and tax-efficient. Take into account instruments including wills, trusts, gifting strategies, and charitable bequests to accomplish legacy objectives.

3- Education and preparation: Make sure the heirs have the information, abilities, and morals required to uphold and expand the family heritage by including provisions for financial education, mentorship, and preparation for handling inherited money.

Sub-chapter 5: Reflections on an Abundant Lifestyle

- **Appreciation Practices**

1- Daily Reflections: Develop a daily practice of thankfulness by thanking God for everything in your life—the plethora of chances, resources, and relationships—by thinking back on your successes and moments of abundance.

2- Gratitude journaling: By recording and celebrating good times, heartfelt conversations, and deeds of kindness, you can cultivate an attitude of plenty, satisfaction, and appreciation for life's benefits.

3- Gratitude Rituals: Include acts of kindness and generosity within the family, express gratitude before bedtime, and share thankfulness throughout mealtimes as examples of gratitude rituals that you can incorporate into your daily routines or traditions.

- **Reviewing a Life Well-Lived**

1- Life Review: Take some time to consider the major turning points, victories, and contributions you have made throughout your life. Celebrate your successes, overcome your obstacles, and show gratitude for the journey you have taken and the lessons you have learned along the way.

2- Legacy Impact: Take into account how financial choices, investments, and charitable activities affect one's happiness, the prosperity of one's family, and constructive contributions to society. This will help you realize how important it is to leave a long-lasting legacy of abundance and empowerment.

3- Future Aspirations: Consider your future self and future generations' needs and ambitions to continue growing, fulfilling your life, and leaving a lasting legacy. Picture a future full of prosperity, significance, and significant influence.

- **Preparing for the Next Generation**

1- Education and Mentorship: Provide heirs access to mentorship, financial education, and practical wealth management expertise so they may confidently carry on the family heritage and make well-informed decisions.

2- Values Transmission: Make sure that the heirs comprehend the significance of moral behavior, societal effects, and upholding family values for future generations by instilling fundamental values, principles, and beliefs about wealth management, responsibility, and service to others.

3- Empowerment and Trust: Give the heirs of the family ownership of the legacy, decision-making power, and responsibilities. This will enable them to take charge of their financial destiny, make their own decisions, and contribute to the family's continued prosperity.

CONCLUSION

In conclusion, obtaining financial mastery is more than just accumulating wealth; it is about developing a mentality and applying tactics that lead to long-term financial freedom and empowerment. Throughout this course, we've looked at a wide range of ways to build wealth and achieve financial independence. From mindful spending and investment strategies to legacy building and ethical investing, each chapter offers useful insights and specific steps for people on their path to financial mastery.

- **Reflect on Financial Mastery**

<u>The key strategies for unlocking money and achieving financial freedom include:</u>
1- **Mindful Spending:** Developing aware consumption habits and matching spending with personal ideals to maximize usefulness while minimizing waste.
2- **Investment Mastery:** Using compounding, diversification, and risk management to build wealth and achieve long-term financial goals.
3- **Maximizing Income Streams:** Looking for options outside of the standard 9-to-5 employment,

negotiating effectively, and exploring entrepreneurial projects to boost earnings.

4- Debt management involves understanding various types of debt, putting debt repayment methods into action, and strategically exploiting credit to develop wealth.

5- Tax Efficiency and Wealth Preservation: Improving tax methods, estate planning, and wealth protection measures to protect and grow assets over time.

6- Behavioral finance mastery entails recognizing and reducing cognitive biases, establishing and accomplishing financial goals, and using decision-making frameworks to make educated decisions.

7- Legacy Building and Impactful Wealth: Defining personal legacies beyond financial wealth, participating in philanthropic and social impact efforts, and passing on financial wisdom to future generations.

- **Call to Action**

I encourage each reader to take action and use the principles mentioned in this guide. Whether you start a savings plan, diversify your investments, or look into new income streams, each action you take puts you closer to financial independence. Share your triumphs with others, motivating them to go on their path to financial mastery and creating a community of support and encouragement along the way.

- ## Continuous Learning

Financial mastery is a journey, not a destination. It necessitates ongoing learning, adaptability, and development. Stay curious, seek out new information, and be open to shifting ideas and best practices in the ever-changing personal finance market. By investing in your financial education, you provide yourself with the tools and insights you need to overcome obstacles, grasp opportunities, and achieve your financial goals.

- ## Financial Freedom Celebration

Finally, take a moment to recognize how far you've come on your path to financial independence and empowerment. Recognize your accomplishments, the challenges you overcame, and the lessons you acquired along the way. Celebrate not only the destination but also the milestones reached and the progress experienced along the way. With determination, discipline, and a commitment to lifelong learning, you may unlock wealth, attain financial freedom, and create an abundant and fulfilling future.

www.ingramcontent.com/pod-product-compliance
Lightning Source LLC
Chambersburg PA
CBHW050106230526
45470CB00004B/1705